Understanding Media:
Inside Celebrity

Edited by Jessica Evans and David Hesmondhalgh

Open University Press
in association with The Open University

Open University Press
McGraw-Hill Education
McGraw-Hill House
Shoppenhangers Road
Maidenhead
Berkshire
England
SL6 2QL

email: enquiries@openup.co.uk
world wide web: www.openup.co.uk

and Two Penn Plaza, New York, NY 10121-2289, USA

First published 2005

A catalogue record of this book is available from the British Library

ISBN 0 335 21881 4 (hb) 0 335 21880 6 (pb)

Library of Congress Cataloguing-in-Publication Data

CIP data applied for

Edited and designed by The Open University.

Typeset by Aldens

Printed and bound in the United Kingdom by Aldens Press.

1.1

Understanding Media:
Inside Celebrity

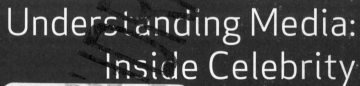

This book is part of a series published by Open University Press in association with The Open University. The complete list of books in this series is as follows:

Understanding Media: Inside Celebrity (editors: Jessica Evans and David Hesmondhalgh)
Media Audiences (editor: Marie Gillespie)
Media Production (editor: David Hesmondhalgh)
Analysing Media Texts (editors: Marie Gillespie and Jason Toynbee)

This publication forms part of an Open University course *Understanding Media* (DA204). Details of this and other Open University courses can be obtained from the Student Registration and Enquiry Service, The Open University, Milton Keynes, MK7 6YG, United Kingdom: tel. +44 (0)1908 653231, email general-enquiries@open.ac.uk.

Alternatively, you may visit The Open University website at http://www.open.ac.uk where you can learn more about the wide range of courses and packs offered at all levels by The Open University.

To purchase a selection of Open University course materials visit http://www.ouw.co.uk, or contact Open University Worldwide, Michael Young Building, Walton Hall, Milton Keynes MK7 6AA, United Kingdom for a brochure. tel. +44 (0)1908 858785; fax +44 (0)1908 858787; email ouwenq@open.ac.uk

Contents

The Open University Course Team

Tony Aldgate, Arts Faculty Advisor
Geoff Austin, Leading Technical Developer
Hedley Bashforth, Associate Lecturer and Study Guide Author
Melanie Bayley, Media Project Manager
Tony Bennett, Chapter Author
Chris Bissell, Chapter Author, Faculty of Technology
Kathleen Calder, Editorial Media Developer
Elizabeth Chaplin, Associate Lecturer and Study Guide Author
James Chapman, Reading Member
Giles Clark, Publishing Advisor
Richard Collins, Chapter Author and Book Editor
Lene Connolly, Print Buying Controller
Shanti Dass, Editorial Media Developer
Alison Edwards, Editorial Media Developer
Jessica Evans, Chapter Author and Book Editor
Tot Foster, Consultant Producer, Sound & Vision
Marie Gillespie, Deputy Course Chair, Chapter Author and Book Editor
Richard Golden, Production and Presentation Administrator
R. Harindranath, Critical Reader, 2002–3
Lisa Hale, Media Assistant, Compositor
Alma Hales, Rights Advisor
Celia Hart, Picture Researcher
David Herbert, Chapter Author & Arts Faculty Advisor
David Hesmondhalgh, Course Chair, Chapter Author and Book Editor
Jonathan Hunt, Publishing Advisor
Denise Janes, Course Secretary, 2002–3
Tim Jordan, Critical Reader, 2002–3
Wendy Lampert, Course Manager
Sylvia Lay-Flurrie, Course Secretary
Alex Law, Associate Lecturer and Study Guide Author
Hugh Mackay, Staff Tutor, Teaching Advisor and Critical Reader
Margaret McManus, Media Assistant, Rights
Katie Meade, Contracts Executive
Diane Mole, Graphics Media Developer
Dave Morris, Interactive Media Developer
Martin Moloney, Associate Lecturer and Study Guide Author
Jason Toynbee, Chapter Author and Book Editor

Consultant Authors

Frances Bonner, University of Queensland
Gill Branston, Cardiff University
Nick Couldry, London School of Economics and Political Science
John Downey, Loughborough University
Jostein Gripsrud, University of Bergen
Sonia Livingstone, London School of Economics and Political Science
Nick Stevenson, University of Nottingham
Gill Ursell, Trinity and All Saints College, University of Leeds

External Assessors

Ann Gray, University of Lincoln
Peter Golding, Loughborough University

Series preface

Understanding Media: Inside Celebrity is the first of four books in a series, also entitled *Understanding Media*. The aim of the series is to provide a cogent and wide-ranging introduction to the study of the media. These four books form the central part of an Open University course with the same title (course code DA204). Each volume is self-contained and can be studied on its own, or as part of a wide range of courses in universities and colleges.

The four books in this series are as follows:

Understanding Media: Inside Celebrity, edited by Jessica Evans and David Hesmondhalgh

Media Audiences, edited by Marie Gillespie

Media Production, edited by David Hesmondhalgh

Analysing Media Texts, edited by Marie Gillespie and Jason Toynbee (with DVD-ROM)

The first book introduces four elements central to any investigation of the media (history, texts, production and audiences) via an analysis of the important media phenomenon of celebrity. The next three books in the series then examine texts, production and audiences in greater detail. Across these different topics, the course addresses three *themes* in media analysis, which the course team believe are fundamental to any appreciation of the importance and complexity of the media. These are

- power
- change and continuity
- knowledge, values and beliefs

These elements and themes can be traced via the index of each book, but the book introductions and conclusions will also help follow how they are pursued across the series.

Understanding Media covers a great deal of media studies curriculum, but of course it still isn't possible for us to cover everything. Nevertheless we have aimed to cover a wide range of media examples, both historically and geographically, and to introduce a number of differing and often competing approaches.

The chapters are designed to be rigorous but student-friendly, and we have sought to achieve this in a number of ways. We have provided clear outlines of the aims of each chapter at its beginning, and summaries at the end, with careful explanations along the way. Activities are built into the chapters, and are designed to help readers understand and retain the key concepts of the course. Just under half of these activities are based around *readings* – extracts drawn from books, academic articles and the media themselves – which are integral to the discussion contained in the chapter. These readings are indicated by a coloured line next to the margin. Each book is thoroughly indexed, so that key concepts can be tracked across the different books in the series. Further reading is indicated at the end of each chapter. Finally, although each book is self-contained, references to other books in the series are indicated by the use of bold type.

A fifth book used on DA204 *Understanding Media* has been published by The Open University alone. This book, entitled *Media Technologies, Markets and Regulation*, is edited by Richard Collins and Jessica Evans and is available from OU Worldwide on +44 (0)1908 858785 (http://www.ouw.co.uk).

Media studies has taken its place as a familiar academic discipline in schools and universities, embraced in large numbers by students, but crassly dismissed by commentators who in most cases seem never to have read a serious analysis of the media. The need to think carefully about the media's role in modern societies is as great as ever. We hope that you find these books a stimulating introduction to this vitally important area of study.

Open University courses are produced by course teams. These teams include academic authors, from The Open University and from other institutions, experienced tutors, External Assessors, editors, designers, audio and video producers, administrators and secretaries. The Open University academics on the *Understanding Media* course team were based mainly in the Sociology discipline, within the Faculty of Social Sciences, but we also drew upon the expertise of colleagues in the Faculty of Arts, in order to construct a course with interdisciplinary foundations and appeal. While book editors have had primary responsibility for each book, the assignment of editors' names to books cannot adequately convey the collective nature of production at The Open University. The names of the *Understanding Media* course team are listed at the front of this book.

I'd like to thank all my colleagues on the course team for their hard work and good humour, especially Wendy Lampert, who has been a really excellent and efficient Course Manager.

David Hesmondhalgh, Course Chair
On behalf of the *Understanding Media* course team

Celebrity: what's the media got to do with it?

Jessica Evans

Famous faces and bodies greet us at every turn. These 'celebrities' appear to be given more media attention, and therefore public recognition, than others. They also seem to have more power than the less visible parts of the population. And if the viewing and circulation figures of the popular print and broadcast media are anything to go by, many of us cannot resist the pleasures gained from simply looking at pictures of celebrities. To the extent that we recognise ourselves in the perspectives offered by the mass media, our ordinary identifications with celebrities seem to be highly ambivalent. [We are fascinated by them and idealise them. At the same time we also envy them, even gaining a certain pleasure from wishing them to fail. Either way, many seem to believe in celebrities and invest in them emotionally.]

This interest in celebrity, at least on the part of the media, leads us to ask some important questions:

- Does a person become a celebrity because they have a special talent?
- Have there always been celebrities?
- To what extent is celebrity a media phenomenon?
- Why do the media promote celebrity?
- What work goes into the making of celebrities?
- With which social values and beliefs are celebrities associated?
- Why are audiences attracted to celebrities?

Why study celebrity?

In this book, we investigate these questions, in particular focusing on the relationship of celebrity with the media. Our response to the first question sums up the premise of this book, for, if there is one central myth of stardom and celebrity that we wish to question, it is that charisma is the cause rather than the effect of fame. We show that individuals do not become celebrities as a result of their innately alluring or magnetic qualities. Rather, celebrity is a resource created and deployed by a range of often interlocking media – such as the press, films and television programmes – to which audiences respond in all manner of ways. Moreover, celebrities are by definition the few, known by the many.

It follows that people can only achieve fame or become celebrities in the first place through the active construction and transmission of an image or persona that represents them.

But why have we selected the topic of celebrity in order to introduce the study of the media? There are three main reasons. First, as has already been implied, celebrity and the media are mutually constitutive. The study of celebrity, of *public* personalities, leads us directly into an analysis of the media, and in particular asks us to account for the fact that the media invest huge resources in the promotion and coverage of celebrity. We consider how celebrity becomes a powerful force in the media, driving the media ideologically and economically. But we show, too, how the source of celebrity power also lies with audiences, for ultimately celebrities are given or lent meaning by viewers, listeners and readers. Second, mass media images and representations of famous people, stars and celebrities are vehicles for the creation of social meanings. A celebrity always represents something more than him- or herself. So celebrity conveys, directly or indirectly, particular social values, such as the meaning of work and achievement, and definitions of sexual and gendered identity (Dyer, 1986; Marshall, 1997). In 'housing' the values, beliefs and norms of the day, celebrity coverage in the media – in newspapers, advertisements, films, television and so on – plays an essential role in organising our perception of the world. Third, since the late 1990s celebrity has become a particularly intense object of interest in the media. It seems to have increasingly provided a focus not only for features and publicity, but also for news and current affairs coverage. As a consequence, there is now a debate, taking place both in the media and academia, about the social significance and effects of celebrity and the extent to which it is a welcome development. It is important to recognise that, going back to the ancient and early Christian periods, there has always been unease about the ethics of fame and its ability to corrupt both individuals and public life (see Braudy, 1986). But in recent years the critical analysis of celebrity has focused on how the mass media set the terms and conditions for conduct in public life (Marshall, 1997; Corner and Pels, 2003).

One of the first writers to consider these points is the much-cited US cultural historian Daniel Boorstin (1961). It is worth saying a little about him, as he helped to frame the debate on 'celebrity culture' that has emerged recently. He claims that images and appearances, the *way* things are presented, have become more important than the substance of a message. The 'graphic revolution' of the twentieth century – the steam press, photographic half-tone reproduction, film and television, all of which led to the widespread reproduction of images – has brought about the rise of what Boorstin calls the 'pseudo-event'. By this he means not only an event staged precisely in order to be disseminated by the media, but also one that is reported before it happens. Celebrity in the twentieth century, Boorstin is perhaps the first to argue, is the quintessential media pseudo-event (1961, p.75). He takes a dim view of today's 'fabricated' celebrities which, compared to the true heroes of a past age, he regards as talentless opportunists. They rely completely on the media industries and their publicity machine to achieve celebrity status. What makes a star is a 'publicisable personality'; a real hero, in contrast, is by definition unsung (1961, p.85). Boorstin's reading of fame usefully highlights one prominent attitude towards celebrity. Ultimately, for Boorstin, modern mass media celebrity is superficial – no celebrity possesses anything real in a culture devoted to consumption. All celebrities are interchangeable.

Whatever one's view of Boorstin's critique, his work has had the great benefit of highlighting the politics of mediated celebrity. More recently, media sociologists from a range of perspectives have argued that mediated celebrity and the values associated with it are altering the conduct of political life (Gitlin, 1998, p.83; Corner and Pels, 2003; Lumby, 1999). For example, when celebrity footballer David Beckham goes to Johannesburg to meet Nelson Mandela or Arnold Schwarzenegger becomes Governor of California, these are indeed political events. However they are also largely orchestrated for the media, and some are pseudo-events, to use Boorstin's term. Moreover, it is a much remarked feature of recent times that there has been a decline of interest in elections and an electoral apathy, particularly amongst younger voters. Conversely, television talent-show contests have audiences rushing to telephone in their vote and determine the winner. In this 'voting paradox', the final two contestants on the *Pop Idol* show (ITV) in February 2002 polled more phone votes than the Liberal Democrats in the 2001 general election (Corner and Pels, 2003, p.1). At the same time, it is said that politics increasingly resembles a talent show in which the personal lives of politicians and their personalities are uppermost in public debate (Corner and Pels, 2003, p.2; Gitlin, 1991, p.120). Whether you think this is a good or a bad thing, or indeed whether you think this is a new development (see Chapter 1), it seems as if entertainment values have to some extent intruded on the sphere of politics. For some, this is evidence that celebrity is the epitome of the 'trivialisation' of the media (Franklin, 1997); for others, mediated celebrity has positive political and democratic benefits (Lumby, 1999). Whatever view you hold of the meaning and impact of celebrity today, it seems true that celebrity raises contentious issues; it exposes questions about the quality of political and public life and the attachments we have to deep-seated values and beliefs underpinning it.

As has already been indicated, in this book we use celebrity as a means of setting out some of the debates and key concepts that any student of the media needs in order to describe, analyse and explain what the media are, how they function, and what effects they have. These practices and processes are often invisible to us as ordinary viewers, listeners and readers of the media, so we aim our spotlight at these backstage areas. Our focus throughout is double-edged: we consider not only the ways in which *particular* celebrities are produced, represented and received, but also how the *concept* of celebrity or 'stars' changes over time and across different media.

We end this section with a note on the concepts of 'stars' and 'celebrities'. Although we now happily refer to 'celebrity' as a category, it is useful to recognise the historical evolution of studies in this area. The first theorisations of what used largely to be termed 'stars' came from early film studies writings (see Dyer, 1986) rather than from the discipline of media studies that evolved later on. 'Celebrity' is a larger category than 'star', for it encompasses the huge range of people whose image circulates without being attached to their initial professional role (whether this be actor, presenter, criminal, politician and so on). So a newsreader becomes a 'celebrity' when appearing as a chat-show guest, for example. Whether the distinction between star and celebrity (the preferred term today) implies a major historical shift so that the specialist, enduring and less attainable 'stars' of the past have been supplanted by all-purpose, mundane and fleeting 'celebrities' of the present, cannot be determined in advance of close historical analysis (see Chapter 1). In any case, we continue to refer to a particular sub-set of celebrities as 'stars' in this book. This is to acknowledge the persistence of the term in the public world where stars are defined in terms of their work in a specific medium (for example, people are referred to as 'film stars' and 'pop stars' rather than film and pop celebrities).

What are the media?

So far, the concept of the 'media' has been used in rather loose terms. In order to assess the role of the media in relation to celebrity, it is important to have a working understanding of this term. What is often termed 'the media' is in fact a diverse array of institutions and practices that have the function, amongst others, of *mediation*. It is useful to think a little about the meaning of media, the plural of medium. In its original Latin it means 'middle' and 'means', which suggests a further definition as an 'intermediate agency' (OED). Mediation suggests an initial separation between two things that can then *become connected* through an intervening substance. Mediation, then, involves the relaying of events or phenomena that we cannot directly observe by ourselves, and it therefore involves a technical medium. So, for example, a telephone allows people to have a conversation without having to share the same physical space –

we can say the telephone mediates between them. John B. Thompson (1995), a British media theorist, argues that in this way the communications media change the relationship between time and space. A whole series of media – from the postal service, to the telegraph, telephone and now email – has meant that time is in general less constrained by space. Thompson (1995) places these forms of mediated communication in the category of *mediated interaction*: they involve the use of a technical medium to transmit information or symbolic content between individuals who are distant from each other. What allows this mediation to occur is the application of a tool or instrument (a medium) to enhance perception and extend our interactions with others.

Over the last few centuries, subsequent to the industrial revolution and the use of mechanisation to produce communication, there has been an unfolding series of technologies that have combined to produce a variety of modes of mediated communication. But, as many media theorists such as Thompson have noted, in the twentieth century the media consolidated around a one-to-many, largely non-*interactive* set of technologies and institutions – such as radio, cinema, print media (books, newspapers, magazines) and television. The kinds of relationship between sender and recipient uniquely established by these centralised media of mass communication differ in some important ways from the two-way mediated interaction of telephones and email. Thompson attributes the following characteristics to mass communications (1995, pp.23–31):

■ They are produced in principle for an indefinite range of potential recipients, a scattered 'general public'.

■ They are not aimed at specific others who are required to produce a more or less immediate response.

■ They are asymmetrical: transmission of messages tends to be one-way and normally structured by a one-to-many model.

■ They are mechanically or digitally recorded and reproducible, have a high degree of fixity, are standardised and infinitely repeatable.

■ They involve the institutionalisation of the means of production and diffusion; that is, the development of mass communications is inseparable from the development of *media industries*, which commercially exploit technological innovations.

Taken together, these characteristics profoundly alter the dissemination of mediated communications. A communication can be fixed, made to endure over time and be infinitely reproduced. Typically, it is produced by an organised group of professional media personnel who are separated by place and time from a relatively much larger and dispersed group of receivers – the audience. Readers or viewers do not directly produce the content and format of a national newspaper or a television programme.

It is on this basis that some media theorists refer to the inherent power imbalance when a group of centralised media producers, often part of vast media organisations (from Time Warner and Murdoch's News Corporation to the BBC), determine what the majority of people get for their media diet every day (see Golding and Murdock, 2000). Others stress how mass communications make audience members feel that they have something in common with each other. As people stand around their workplace water-cooler they talk about the latest headlines or the latest celebrity scandal; hence mass communications make the world 'talkable about by everyone' (Scannell, 1989, p.152). So, media representations give celebrities a ubiquitous presence to such an extent that we may feel we come to know them intimately. This returns us to the importance of mediation, for communicative artefacts supply images and symbols that people use to mediate, or make sense of, their social environment. Celebrities play a key role in this process because they supply a human dimension to the public world, personifying or personalising things that may otherwise be quite abstract. This makes those things easier to identify with, simpler and quicker to understand (see, for example, Chapter 1, Section 4.2).

The structure of this book

As we have seen, one commentator, Boorstin, argues that celebrities typify pseudo-events – they are trivial and empty of meaning. This way of thinking belongs to a tradition that regards celebrity as part of a culture 'industry' (Adorno and Horkheimer, 1979/1944). In this view, sometimes called the 'mass culture' approach, celebrity is 'manufactured' just as other industries manufacture clothing or process foods. Celebrities, it is argued, are subsumed under a larger and impersonal system of capitalist production. Part of an industrial scale of rationalisation and standardisation, celebrity is yet another commodity for mass consumption. But, according to its many critics, this approach is essentially *reductive* (Dyer, 1979, p.13; see Jensen, 1984). It is reductive because it claims that celebrity and celebrities are not worth studying in themselves, for their meaning is determined in advance by an abstracted system – 'capitalism' – which is seen as having its own needs and laws. Nor do the ways in which audiences interpret or identify with celebrities bear much analysis. For the 'mass culture' advocates think of audiences' responses to celebrities in terms of supply and demand. Audiences' 'consumption' is, then, merely a spontaneous effect of economic supply. Given this, it is perhaps not surprising that the mass culture critics did not investigate the content of celebrity representations, nor consider how individual celebrities were created and disseminated by organisations and received by particular audiences in their historical contexts (Dyer, 1986, p.13).

In this book we investigate the areas often ignored by mass culture critics. In so doing we have organised the chapters into four main themes. Chapter 1 develops a critical engagement with the claim of some theorists that there is something unique today which can be called 'celebrity culture'. In particular it assesses the strengths and weaknesses of two perspectives on celebrity culture that share this view, which are termed 'democratic-populist' and 'cultural decline'. It is argued that, while it is important to be sensitive to recent historical changes in the meaning and impact of celebrity, equally we must not lose sight of some of the important continuities between past and present. For example, we see how the themes in present-day representations of celebrity – the great interest in celebrities' personal lives, for example – have their precedents as far back as the nineteenth century. Finally, the chapter takes the relationship between modern politics and the mass media as a case study. It is suggested that while neither public relations nor pseudo-events are unique to the period of the mass media, politics today may be becoming 'celebritised'. Depending on whether you take the cultural decline or populist view, this may have the effect of making politics less elitist and more accessible, or it may overly simplify and trivialise political life.

One function of the media, as has already been mentioned, is to mediate the world to us, its audiences. It does this by representing the world in textual artefacts (magazines, films, television programmes and so on). In texts, the world 'out there' is *actively* 'made up' in words and images. We stress 'actively' because there remains a widespread belief that texts are merely *re*-presentations or reflections of a reality located somewhere else. However, texts, the subject of Chapter 2, do not simply reflect the world or reproduce meanings already embedded in objects or events, but rather *transform* that world for readers, listeners and viewers. As you will see in Chapter 2, one reason why the concept of *text* has been useful as a way of analysing media content is because it can cover a fusion of visual, auditory and written elements in any one media message. Texts, whether they are a television programme, a magazine article or a website, are the things that *link* the activities of producers and audiences. In texts, meanings are 'encoded' or created for celebrities that shape the way in which viewers, readers and listeners will 'decode' or interpret them. Chapter 2 shows why texts deserve consideration in their own right: they involve conventions such as stereotypes that construct celebrities in terms of existing beliefs about, for example, gender or 'race'. The chapter sets out how celebrity is used to organise and promote different kinds of media texts and group them together – by genre, for example. Finally, picking up on the debate about 'celebritisation', discussed in Chapter 1, the chapter considers how an analysis of media content can provide evidence for the increase in presence of celebrity in news media.

While Chapter 2 looks at the communicative structures of media texts, Chapter 3 turns our attention to the internal procedures and organisational structures of media institutions that promotes celebrity and produces individual celebrities. But there are a number of ways of conceptualising production, and the chapter compares three of them: organisational sociology, political economy and post-structuralism. Each makes different assumptions about which aspect of production is most important in determining the media products we get. The sociology of organisations focuses in detail on the actual ways in which media personnel, whether they are picture editors or PR companies, go about their work. It tells us how everyday working practices within institutional settings feed into the creative process. In contrast, political economy looks at media more as an industry and focuses on the macro contexts of production – the economic pressures on, and strategies used by, the often profit-making organisations that dominate media markets. Finally, the post-structuralist approach emphasises how celebrities – because they have special properties of visibility – are uniquely placed to embody the fantasies of the population as a whole and, in particular, represent the kinds of individuals we should be. Celebrity, as a key part of the mass entertainment industry, has a function of regulating the relationships between those who disseminate media products and their audiences.

As Thompson argues (1995, p.29), mass communication involves a structured 'break' between producers and receivers. One implication of this is that although broadcasters and other media producers may *intend* certain messages to be communicated successfully to their recipients, the latter in reality actively interpret texts in a variety of ways. Chapter 4 focuses on this domain of *reception*, on how celebrities provide a focus for the fantasies and pleasures of movie-goers, magazine readers and other media audiences. While Chapter 3 considers the economic and social forces and organisations that manufacture stars, causing them to exist in the first place, Chapter 4 accounts for how particular audiences and individual viewers may identify with celebrities and consequently may shape their meaning or find their own meanings in them. As we will see, the gender or class affiliations of audience members shape the kind of pleasure given by a particular media text. A range of approaches to reception is discussed, from those that analyse media texts and make assumptions about audience response based on this analysis, to those involving the empirical study – through interview techniques, for example – of actual audience members. Audiences may 'resist' the meanings that producers intend or they may identify with celebrities in order to resolve underlying psychological conflicts. When we look at audiences' tangible 'uses' of celebrities we find that a range of readings and identifications may exist.

We want to emphasise throughout the book how each element – text, production and audience reception – contributes in its own way to making celebrity a meaningful social entity. In reality, however, these processes of text, production and reception do not necessarily operate as separate areas of activity. In the conclusion to the book we return to this point, but all you need do here is to note that these aspects of mediated celebrity have been separated for reasons of analytical clarity. We think each requires special theoretical and empirical attention in its own right, even though they are, of course, interdependent in many ways.

References

Adorno, T. and Horkheimer, M. (1979/1944) 'The culture industry: enlightenment as mass deception' in Adorno, T. and Horkheimer, M. (eds) *Dialectic of Enlightenment*, London, Verso.

Boorstin, D. (1961) *The Image: A Guide to Pseudo-Events in America*, Harmondsworth, Penguin.

Braudy, L. (1986) *Frenzy of Renown*, New York, Vintage Books.

Corner, J. and Pels, D. (eds) (2003) *Media and the Restyling of Politics*, London, Sage.

Dyer, R. (1979) *Stars*, London, BFI Publishing. (Reprinted in 2001.)

Dyer, R. (1986) *Heavenly Bodies: Film Stars and Society*, London, BFI Publishing.

Franklin, B. (1997) *Newszak and News Media*, London, Edward Arnold.

Gitlin, T. (1991) 'Bites and blips' in Dahlgren, P. and Sparks, C. (eds) *Communication and Citizenship*, London, Routledge.

Gitlin, T. (1998) 'The culture of celebrity', *Dissent*, Summer, pp.81–3.

Golding, P. and Murdock, G. (2000) 'Culture, communications and political economy' in Curran, J. and Gurevitch, M. (eds) *Mass Media and Society* (3rd edn), London, Edward Arnold.

Jensen, J. (1984) 'An interpretive approach to cultural production' in Rowland, W. and Watkins, B. (eds) *Interpreting Television*, London, Sage.

Lumby, C. (1999) *Gotcha: Life in a Tabloid World*, Sydney, Allen and Unwin.

Marshall, P.D. (1997) *Celebrity and Power: Fame in Contemporary Society*, Minneapolis, MN, University of Minnesota Press.

Scannell, P. (1989) 'Public service broadcasting and modern public life', *Media, Culture and Society*, vol.11, pp.135–66.

Thompson, J.B. (1995) *The Media and Modernity*, Cambridge, Polity Press.

Celebrity, media and history

Chapter 1

Jessica Evans

Contents

1   Some perspectives on 'celebrity culture'

It seems that a significant amount of the media information we use to learn about the world involves celebrities. Moreover, it is often said that we live in a culture that is uniquely – unlike past cultures – dominated by celebrities.

Activity 1.1

Look at Plate 1 in the colour section. Observe all the elements assembled to constitute this image, including lighting, pose, facial expression, camera angle and composition. What kind of man do you think this is?

Now look at Plate 9 in the colour section. This is the front cover of an issue of the US weekly magazine, *Newsweek* from 1995. Have your views about the man in Plate 1 changed? How does the front cover of this magazine represent (portray) this man? You might want to look at Plate 10 too. ■ ■ ■

Newsweek is a US mass circulation magazine. The entire front cover of this issue is taken up by a picture of a man whom you may recognise without the help of the headlines in Plate 9. It is Timothy McVeigh, who was executed for the bombing of the Oklahoma City Federal building in April 1995 that killed 167 people. What is interesting about this cover and the story it relates (set out in Plate 10 – do not bother trying to read the text of the article unless you want to, simply look at the layout) is that, through them, McVeigh has been subjected to a process of *celebritisation* (see Gabler in Sturken, 2001). Of course, he was already well known nationally and internationally, because there was inevitably great interest in the crime for which he was responsible. In using the term 'celebritisation', however, we refer to something else: the fact that *Newsweek* has used various 'devices' to portray McVeigh as a personality, a distinctive individual, even a glamorous person. The visual and verbal elements that create meaning in this photograph of McVeigh – the pose, lighting, camera angle, composition, facial expression, headlines and written copy – are all particular textual devices. They have been selected and combined together to convey a particular meaning. If other kinds of lighting or a different pose, another caption, had been used instead, the effect (the overall meaning) could have been quite different. These textual devices (which are discussed further in Chapter 2) do the work of shaping the meaning of events or people, directing readers and viewers to make sense of these events in one way rather than another.

Celebritisation, then, is the process in which someone is turned into a celebrity, or to put it more strongly, the process in which celebrity is fabricated. This, I will argue in this chapter, is a process of considerable social and even political significance. In the case of McVeigh, by using various devices, viewers are encouraged to feel an intimacy with him. Indeed, he could almost be mistaken for a film star. We look at him in close-up, as if we are peering into his soul; he stares into the distance with a penetrating look as if in profound thought. This is not the police mug-shot usually deployed for criminal suspects; rather, with its subtle tonal range and attention to facial features, this cover obeys the portrait conventions that flatter a subject. When you turned to Plate 9, did you find that the headline 'The suspect speaks' jarred with this 'positive' image of McVeigh. Without this headline it is highly unlikely you would have realised that McVeigh was a criminal suspect unless, of course, you had already recognised him. In the triplet of images in Plate 10 McVeigh is asked to pose by the photographer and larks about, trying on different poses. The journalist tells us that McVeigh was actually photographed inside the El Reno Federal Correctional Institution – but for the purposes of the photograph he is placed in a new context. It is as if the prison has been turned into a photographer's studio! This seems likely to persuade us to think of McVeigh as less like a mere criminal and more like an interesting person, even a celebrity, in his own right. On the inside pages, there is a detailed interview with McVeigh, who speaks about his parents' divorce, his childhood, girlfriends and his life in the army. He comes across overwhelmingly as a 'normal' all-American boy who had a love for his country and did a spell in the US military as a way of 'discovering' himself (*Newsweek*, 1995, p.27).

The importance placed on every utterance by McVeigh in the accompanying article and the overall amplification of his personality, through the textual devices discussed earlier, is typical of the way in which individuals are portrayed as celebrities. Thus, McVeigh is made to appear as a unique individual with distinctive qualities and personal history. One possible reason for the celebritisation of McVeigh is that he was an ex-army man, young and white, and a patriot (Sanchez in Sturken, 2001). In the *Newsweek* story, his earlier experiences of patriotic army service and military action abroad are seen as an almost natural preparation for the act he committed in Oklahoma. The overall impression given by the article is that he is one of America's 'sons' who took an accidental turning in life (Gabler in Sturken, 2001). At the least, it appears that this article is ambivalent about McVeigh's status as a terrorist and in some ways portrays him as a hero, or at least as someone who deserves respect. Perhaps this is a measure of the extent to which the *Newsweek* organisation – whether we understand this as its journalists' or proprietor's views or its presumption about its readership (see Chapter 3) – *identifies* with this young American man. That is, unlike other terrorists, such as Islamic fundamentalists, whom the US now and probably for the foreseeable future regard as criminals, McVeigh is treated as someone that US readers are expected to relate to, recognise as one of their own and even empathise with.

This example shows how celebrity coverage in the media actually works as a set of textual devices that convey symbolic meaning, and you will study this in greater detail in Chapter 2. It is a powerful example of how the media portrayal and *construction* of celebrities shape the way in which audiences understand and make sense of the social world. McVeigh is used as a 'peg' to articulate social values and beliefs that may be implicit and unquestioned. It also shows·that the celebritisation process is not as superficial as some proclaim it to be (Boorstin, 1961; see Book Introduction). So, an analysis such as this of celebritisation (the media's manufacture of celebrities) is important in and of itself, and much of this book is devoted to this task. However, some cultural and media theorists use examples of celebritisation to argue for a more significant trend – the *increased prominence* of celebrity in our culture as a whole (Turner et al., 2000; Corner and Pels, 2003; Marshall, 1997). Indeed, they might say that our example of McVeigh is typical of a new cultural shift in which even the most unlikely and inappropriate subjects – criminals – are turned into celebrities and that this is surely a sign of the expansion of celebrity coverage in general. The idea that celebrities dominate contemporary life in new and unprecedented ways is found in the two main perspectives – populist democracy and cultural decline – that I would now like to introduce. Both these perspectives support the idea that celebrity culture is a contemporary or recent phenomenon, but they have rather different approaches to it.

1.1 Celebrity as populist democracy

A number of critics take the view that celebrity culture represents a process of social levelling (Gray, 2002; Cowen, 2000; see also Garratt, 2002; Liddiment, 2003; Frank, 2002) (see Figure 1.1). For them, celebrity culture is the natural end-point of a long process of democratisation and the development of a capitalist market society. They argue that the commercial exploitation of a range of media technologies – the buying and selling of media products in a market – has led to an ever-widening accessibility of these products to the population as a whole (see Hartley, 1996; Thompson, 1995).

Apologists for an unfettered market say it allows audiences themselves to determine who can become celebrities. For example, they argue that in 'reality television' programmes such as *Big Brother* (Channel 4) or *Pop Idol* (ITV), we, the public, are made directly responsible for expressing our preferences by having the power to decide on the winner through our (phone) votes. New electronic media are seen as breakthrough technologies in further enabling a 'DIY' celebrity culture. The internet, for example, has been lauded for widening the pool of potential celebrities by allowing would-be celebrities to sidestep the normal centralised channels of the media industry. It is said to lower the entry barriers, making it far easier – because it is cheaper and faster – to interact with (aspiring) celebrities, creating (and then destroying) them through email chat (Gamson, 2000; see MacManus, 2004). This has increased the number of opportunities for ordinary people to have their '15 minutes of fame', as Andy Warhol once said. Today's 'overnight' celebrities – fashionable today but gone tomorrow – are positive proof of this.

For the populists, fame is part of a western ideal of personal freedom. Today's celebrity culture is based on rewarding self-improvement and efforts towards self-development, rather than being a consequence of hierarchical privilege and elite networks. Celebrity is a positive force for the good because it represents the power of the individual based on characteristics that are unique to that person alone; it therefore represents equality. Accordingly, it is said that each celebrity today has something that is distinctively 'theirs' – you do not even need talent, but simply recognition for what you 'are'. Essentially, you are famous for yourself. For example, celebrity 'wannabes' who take part in television talent shows such as ITV's *Pop Idol* make a virtue of their weaknesses and reinvent their identities, finding a distinctive image that defines them as unique and different from others – on *Pop Idol*, a stammer or being overweight were examples of this (see Garratt, 2002; Braudy, 1997). Hence, fame typifies a particular idea of personal freedom and motivation to succeed that all should share. This view is most frequently expressed by media proprietors, journalists or editors who want to defend their interests in publishing stories about celebrities.

Figure 1.1 'Posh and Becks' cartoon, 1999. This cartoon refers to the wedding of Victoria Adams (ex-member of the Spice Girls pop band) to David Beckham (ex-Manchester United and England football player). 'Posh and Becks', regarded as occupying the ranks of the nouveau riche, were at the time widely referred to as the New Royals, and their mansion was jokily renamed 'Beckingham Palace' in the popular press. The cartoon makes reference to the pictures the Beckhams sold to OK! magazine of their wedding, which was regal and English-historical – a coat of arms, liveried attendants, gold thrones for bride and groom, a crown for the bride, and the use of Princess Diana's jewellers. The Daily Mirror reported it as 'the people's royal wedding'

1.2 Celebrity as cultural decline

Some theorists, critical of the kinds of values represented by celebrity in recent years, hold that celebrity represents a cultural decline, a lapse from an earlier age when fame had a scarcity value (Boorstin, 1961; Walker, 1970; Schickel, 1985; Gitlin, 1998; Postman, 1985; South, 2000). According to Daniel Boorstin (1961), for example, the category of celebrity has widened so much that fame is not an attribution that reflects any real achievement or skill, but rather the success expressed in celebrity is 'success without the requisite association with work' (Marshall, 1997, p.ix). Nowadays, he argues, public recognition is valued for its own sake. Boorstin assumes that at some point in the past fame was legendary and noble, a referential yardstick for virtuous deeds, integrity or honour. It embodied nobler and higher values, such as great thoughts and ideals or services for the higher good. For Boorstin, today's celebrities suffer from narcissistic self-obsession. They stand for a culture where instant gratification is preferred over more long-term rewards and where surface image is valued more than the substance underneath (Postman, 1985; South, 2000). Other theorists point to the erosion of the boundaries that allowed different values to be attached to different social and institutional spheres. These spheres — such as the public and the private, high art and commercial culture, news and entertainment — have become merged and they have come to share the same values and norms of behaviour (Sennett, 1977; Lash, 1990). Politicians are celebritised when the media erode the boundaries between public and private life, obsessively pursuing information about their private lives (such as their sexual relationships and personal views) even if irrelevant to their public role (Corner and Pels, 2003). Moreover, celebrities themselves have real power when their publicists, public relations strategists and agents can exert control over the content of newspapers and magazines (Wells and Twist, 2002; South, 2000; see Turner et al., 2000; see the discussion in Chapter 3, Section 2).

You may have noticed that these two perspectives attach different *values* to celebrity culture: put simply, the first is 'for' and the second is 'against'. But they also share two assumptions. First, celebrity becomes a metaphor for the contemporary condition of society as a whole, whether this condition is one of decline or popular self-expression. Thus, 'celebrity culture' is regarded as expressing a Zeitgeist (from the German 'spirit of the times'). The second assumption is that celebrity has an increased cultural significance today, linked to new cultural values (whether these be increased equality or a decline in standards) that were not present in previous periods.

In this chapter we shall assess the relationship between the media and celebrity over time. One aim is to question the idea that the interest in celebrity and the widespread circulation of celebrities is as definitive of our times, or as new as is claimed. As we will see, change often happens in a small-scale, piecemeal fashion, so that elements of the 'old' are reformulated and combined with new developments.

So we cannot just assume that celebrity is more important or different now than at earlier moments. We need to investigate the *link* between changes in the media and changes in celebrity over time. It is important, therefore, to attend to the individual circumstances of each celebrity phenomenon and understand the meaning of celebrity within the context of its historical moment. Another aim of this chapter is to contrast the populist and cultural decline perspectives of celebrity culture. We will see that each offers a story, but not the whole story, of the meaning of celebrity.

Section 2 introduces a working definition of celebrity as 'mediated persona' in order to emphasise that celebrity is dependent on the media for its existence. We establish that mediation has always been a key aspect of celebrity and that there are significant continuities between past and present representations of celebrity. Section 3 is a case study of an important historical period, 1890 to 1930, in which the mass media (photography, the press and film) created important new ideas about stars. The research used in the section provides a historically nuanced account. It shows how elements of celebrity culture with which we are familiar now, and that are often regarded as recent phenomena, were becoming commonplace a hundred years ago – such as the interest in the private lives of public people. Having considered some of the connections between fame and stardom in the past and today's celebrity culture, Section 4 discusses whether the power and influence of the celebrity system are different and more intense today. It takes the case of mediated celebrity and modern politics, questioning whether politics is becoming fundamentally altered by celebrity culture. We apply the two perspectives we have just outlined – popular democracy (hereafter called the populist perspective) and the cultural decline perspective – in order to assess the strengths and weaknesses of their interpretations of celebrity politics.

2 Celebrity as mediated persona

2.1 What is mediated persona?

> Everyone wants to be Cary Grant. I want to be Cary Grant.
>
> Cary Grant, quoted in McCann, 1996, p.6

What is a celebrity? Celebrities are, of course, *meant* to be remarkable people, who have charismatic appeal and extraordinary qualities – we refer to someone as 'a celebrity' as if that is *essentially* what they are. Think of the metaphor of 'star' – we speak of people who emanate a bright and powerful light. The German sociologist Max Weber (1864–1920) described charisma as one type of social authority and defined the charismatic individual as 'a certain quality of an individual personality by virtue of which he is set apart from ordinary men and treated as endowed with supernatural, superhuman or at least superficially exceptional qualities' (in Dyer, 1979, p.35). But, does this power really emanate from the individual star or celebrity him- or herself? Is the appeal of a celebrity a *consequence* of his or her innate qualities? Is it the living person behind the image whom we see in our magazines and on our television screens who is charismatic? Or is it their image, that later we term 'mediated persona', which makes them seem charismatic?

Activity 1.2

Re-read the quotation at the beginning of the section, taken from a biography of the film star Cary Grant. Make a brief note of what you think this quotation means. ■ ■ ■

In the quotation, Grant seems to imply that a fabrication, albeit one supposedly based on him, is in public circulation. He appears bemused to find that 'Cary Grant' has become an entity unobtainable even to him, almost as if he had nothing to do with it! He can only aspire to achieving Cary Grant-*ness*, since 'his' public character has become a representation stitched together from a number of colourful texts that circulate quite independently of the real, living person called Cary Grant. Again, Grant himself summed up the problem, after his failed marriage to Barbara Hutton, saying that 'She thought that she was marrying Cary Grant'. It probably did not help that even his name was manufactured – in common with many other entertainment stars since the nineteenth century – underlining the fictional basis of his public identity. Grant's birth name, Archibald Leach, was considered by Paramount Studios to be an impediment to a successful film career.

These representations may share a similarity of physical attributes with the material person of Grant, but they are not attributes of him and should not be confused *with* him. If Cary Grant had trouble finding himself among the representations of himself, the attachment of audience members to celebrities can also involve misunderstandings. Entertainment celebrities report that fans write to them commonly confusing them with the characters they play. For images, accompanied by a gossipy style of journalism, can make public people feel very familiar to us. They are endlessly repeated and invade the private spaces of our homes through the mass media. We can easily come to believe that we 'know' the people in these images, perhaps even better than people we spend time with. For some, this impression of intimacy is taken a step further. Some spectators and listeners have passionate love/hate relationships with celebrities – of which the extreme examples are fans and stalkers – and there are well-documented cases of how destructive these attachments can be (Schickel, 1985). Some stalkers and fans seek to break down more actively the gap between themselves and the object of their adoration in order to control or become them (see Chapter 4).

However, it seems difficult, as Grant implied, to close the gap between celebrity and onlooker, to match the person inside with the public image. This seems to be part of the condition of celebrity: celebrities depend for their status and popularity on a larger group of people who observe them and their image from a distance. It therefore follows that any charisma that celebrities possess must be a consequence of the distance from their audience – a distance achieved through the fact that they only appear as representations in mediated texts, however familiar to their audience they seem to be. As a general category, then, celebrity and its charismatic effect are dependent on the lack of a face-to-face relationship. You may remember from the Book Introduction that one key feature of even the most basic communications media is that they involve 'mediated interaction' – using a technical medium to transmit information or symbolic content to individuals who are separated from each other in space and often in time. If celebrities are the few, known by the many, then people can only become celebrities through the transmission of their image: celebrity *by definition* requires mediation.

Celebrity is, therefore, only available by means of texts that circulate to create an image of that person (see Chapter 2). It is the result of creating an image that is only *loosely* attached to a living individual who carries the burden of it – as Grant was only too aware. We can call this image a celebrity's *mediated persona*. Persona (from the Latin, 'persona' for a mask worn by an actor) is the distinctive image of a person built up from the sum of their mediated appearances. It cannot be reduced to the idiosyncrasies of the real embodied person. Nor is it based solely on what we know of someone from a particular film character they play or other professional performance they put on. It combines elements of each of these to form a 'public presence' (Gledhill, 1991, pp.214–15). Rather than being simply a meaning contained within one individual text, such as one film, persona involves the *circulation* of meanings across different media, different genres and different formats. It may involve aspects of typical roles they play, the image they present in interviews and on chat-shows, celebrity 'inside gossip' and so on. Subsequently, someone's persona can change over time (for further discussion see Chapter 2). Mediated persona is a useful term in that it reminds us how celebrity as a category *is absolutely dependent on the media* to create and disseminate a persona to an audience.

2.2 How new is mediated celebrity? Celebrity, continuity and change

So far we have argued that celebrity persona is dependent on and created through the mediating work of the media – a major theme of this book. But, have fame and celebrity *always* been dependent on the media?

According to Boorstin (see Book Introduction), a cultural decline theorist, the gloomy answer is 'no'. He argues that honour and heroism were at some point in the past recognised for what they truly were, *without* public expression through publicity (see Braudy, 1997, p.9). Therefore, it is the modern mass media that have made fame a desirable end in its own right: 'A celebrity is a person who is known for his well-knownness' (Boorstin, 1961, p.57).

However, some historians have cast doubt on the idea that there was such a 'golden age' when acknowledgement and publicity for accomplishment in the public realm was regarded as secondary to the accomplishment itself (Braudy, 1997, p.9). They point out, too, that cultural decline theorists never specify when exactly the golden moment in the past was supposed to have occurred. Leo Braudy, a US cultural historian, argues that fame and the deeds it represents have *always depended on* media management. He questions Boorstin's assumption that heroic deeds and their public expression can ever be separated: how would we ever know they were heroic and valid if we didn't get to hear of them?! Braudy (1997, p.9) thinks that moralists like Boorstin have always made great reputations for books denouncing the desire to be recognised, just as today's preachers evangelise about inner, spiritual truths but choose to do this on television! Moreover, Braudy and others have shown extensively how the urge to fame itself, the desire to be singled out from other human beings for special attention, is not new (Braudy, 1997; Burke, 1992). Other societies in the past have disseminated images of special people for admiration, emulation and fear – be they priests, generals, gods, kings, saints or political leaders – when it was quite clear their achievements were not always worthy or selfless.

So, it can be argued that there is much continuity between the representations of the famous in the past and the present (see Figure 1.2), whatever the method of dissemination (such as coins, photographs, monuments and the internet). To take one example, the use of available media by powerful figureheads in earlier societies was similar to the use of today's media by politicians and state leaders, such as the myriad representations of King Louis XIV (1639–1715) (see Figure 1.3). His advisers aimed to project a triumphal image modelled on Alexander the Great. They gave detailed strictures as to how he was to be posed (Burke, 1992). His image was everywhere, inscribed on clocks, ceilings and furnishings, paintings, tapestries, monuments, sculptures, shop signs and cheap pottery plates, many of which have survived. Some media were mechanically reproducible, thus magnifying the King's visibility: prints (such as engravings and woodcuts) could be made in thousands of copies, medals in hundreds (Burke, 1992, p.16). One historian (Burke, 1992) claims that Louis XIV was a master of the staged 'pseudo-event', a

Figure I.2 *Silver tetradrachm minted by Lysimachus, Greek, 305–281 BC. The earliest known portraits of Alexander the Great are on coins such as these, which were produced during the reign of successors such as Lysimachus in order to cast themselves as his heir. On the front of the coin Alexander is adorned with the ram's horns of Jupiter Ammon, denoting his descent from the Gods*

concept invented by Boorstin to apply to twentieth-century celebrity. What appeared to be spontaneous actions were in fact staged with some care, such as the public rejoicings on the news of French victories.

So there are continuities between the past and present: the media, whether the mass media of the twentieth century or that of the pre-print period, are and always have been essential to celebrity. For, in order to be 'known' by many and talked of at a distance and from afar, one needs a medium of dissemination. And these continuities reach back well before the development of the mass media as we know them today. As we have briefly seen, Louis XIV's period was not devoid of images and representations of the famous, nor was it felt to be at the time. Nor did it lack what we now call 'public relations' or the deliberate attempt to alter the appearance of things (Burke, 1992).

Figure 1.3 *Louis Victorious. Louis at Maastricht by Pierre Mignard, oil on canvas, 1673. Pinacoteca, Turin*

However, there are important differences between past and present too, because different social systems underpin the particular methods of disseminating the images of public figures. Later, we will consider some of the differences between the ways in which monarchs such as Louis XIV and modern-day democratic leaders relate to the media (Section 4.3). However, in general, we can say that under the autocratic political systems of the pre-modern period, visual representations were almost entirely of the great and the powerful. In the period of monarchical power, the visibility of the powerful few was essential to their position at the top of a social hierarchy. Thus, public appearances were carefully staged, full of pomp and ritual that served to underline the exalted power of the monarch, who was the symbolic and actual centre of the social world. Before the nineteenth century, ordinary people rarely attained public visibility and if they did so it was en masse as a collective entity such as the urban crowd, often regarded in derogatory terms as the 'mob'. But, with the process of industrialisation and the increasing enfranchisement of the populace over the eighteenth and nineteenth centuries, new elements of the population were made publicly visible. Fame, albeit unevenly, slowly became associated with social mobility rather than with ascribed or inherited social position. For example, in 1831, a bourgeois Parisian proudly exhibited his painted miniature portrait next to that of King Louis Phillippe with the following inscription: 'There is no real difference between Philippe and me: he is a citizen king and I am a kingly citizen!' (Freund, 1980, p.20). Celebrity or fame is no longer associated with the power to kill, tax or enslave, as it was in the time of monarchs such as Louis XIV or Napoleon.

As we pointed out in Section 1, both the cultural decline and populist perspectives share the observation that fame and celebrity have expanded to include many more 'ordinary' people now than in the past. They both agree that today's celebrity is different from that of past cultures, in that it does not now reflect any heroic or rare achievement. But the difference is that cultural decline theorists tend to mourn the loss of the more inaccessible celebrities of the past and the social values they signified, whereas the populists welcome the expansion of the category of celebrity, a contrast that will be discussed further in Section 4.

3 Inventing the twentieth-century celebrity persona

We have established that fame has always been mediated – represented and disseminated by the media of the day. We noted that celebrity culture existed in previous periods, before the advent of today's mass media, but we emphasised that continuities and change co-exist in the history of mediated fame. In this section, we consider a crucial historical period – 1890–1930 – in which the mass media invented a particular kind of 'star' persona (as it was then termed – see the Book Introduction). During this period some of the central devices of celebritisation with which we are familiar today (such as those discussed at the beginning of Section 1.1) were invented. Over a period of three or four decades, these devices defined the idea of the star in important new ways, although they also built upon the past. What developed at this time, as is emphasised in this section, was the idea that the professional role – the film role or public performance – is an unreliable guide to the nature of the 'real' self. And, therefore, the actor or performer's 'real self', their lifestyles and personalities, must lie *behind* the on-screen life and surpass it in importance (Ponce de Leon, 2002, p.5). By the 1920s, through gossipy accounts and star profiles, the 'private life' of a celebrity had become an essential part of their persona. During this period the popular press created more space for coverage of stars, and entertainment values became more dominant in newspaper journalism.

3.1 The 'human interest' story in popular magazines and newspapers

Before the invention of the film star (see Section 4.2), the emerging mass circulation press of the late 1800s began to cover celebrity and to create celebrities as a result. By the last decade of the nineteenth century, a series of changes in the media of publicity and communication established celebrity as a 'mass' phenomenon. With the invention of the telegraph, the arrival of the rotary press, the founding of the newswire services, and by the late 1880s with the development of the half-tone photographic print, information could move without being impeded by the physical constraints of space (Schudson, 1978). From the 1890s onwards, newspapers and magazines in the US greatly expanded their visual and written coverage of celebrities, adding new forms of human-interest stories and publicising the activities of figures from a wide range of fields, focusing on their home lives, habits and lifestyles. In the UK and the US, between the 1870s and 1890s, there was a proliferation of literary celebrity coverage – where celebrities would be interviewed in the intimate style of a relaxed conversation or 'chat' in their home (Salmon, 1997). For example, the journalist Edmund Yates began his interview with the poet Tennyson, published in his *Celebrities at Home* magazine series (1877–1879) by picturing a 'mansion of welcome solitude away from the haunts of the crowd and safe from the intrusion of the curious' (in Salmon, 1997, p.168). This flattering approach to the reader, implying that s/he alone had a privileged glimpse of the private world of the celebrity (which is paradoxically being put on public show for *all* to see), is the precedent for today's *Hello!* magazine spreads. Newspapers and mass circulation magazines in the US such as *Cosmopolitan* assigned reporters as 'dramatic paragraphers' who produced weekly stories about show business celebrities, including foreign actors such as Sarah Bernhardt, who became international celebrities (Ponce de Leon, 2002, p.208).

Activity 1.3

Look at Figures 1.4, 1.5 and 1.6. Spend a few minutes noting how you think Jennings Bryan, Vanderbilt and Barrymore are represented in these articles. You should consider all the elements including pictures (such as pose and context), headlines and choice of language. ■ ■ ■

In Figures 1.4, 1.5 and 1.6 we have a politician, a society woman and an actor, and in each case they are represented as if their private life is as important to the reader as their public life. There is an emphasis on the reader being able to go behind the scenes, backstage as it were, into the private worlds of their domestic lives – their family and leisure pursuits, aesthetic and lifestyle choices and so on. Although Vanderbilt is an heiress and soon-to-be member of the English aristocracy, she is presented as 'a good, average American girl'. Likewise, Jennings Bryan may be a politician, but he is presented more as a lover of simple American domesticity. These references to domestic life allow for forms of identification between celebrities and their readers – the magazines serve to unmask the *ordinary* person behind the extraordinary public persona and allow the reader an intimate relationship with them. By the end of the nineteenth century, leisure and entertainment values – such as the interest in domestic trivia, private lives and lifestyles – began to vie with the conventions of dispassionate journalism in the popular press (something that is taken up in the discussion of tabloidisation in Chapter 2). Examples include the use of drama, sensational or heightened emotions, and inducements to the readership to find pleasure in identifying with stars and their personal predicaments or lifestyle choices. Magazines such as *The Saturday Evening Post* dispensed with traditional reviews altogether and dedicated itself to long features on stars (Ponce de Leon, 2002, p.208).

3.2 The invention of the 'film star' persona

Although there was a significant dissemination of star images, it is notable that the kinds of entertainment stars covered by newspapers at this time were from theatre and vaudeville. The medium of film was not yet associated with stars and therefore there was no conception of a 'film star'. We can say that there was no *discourse* of the film star; that is, there was no way of speaking of such an entity, no accounts circulating about it. As a consequence, no such thing as a 'film star' could exist in public life or in the minds of the public at this time. This is where the important historical research of US film historian Richard deCordova (1990) comes in. Using industry documents, deCordova shows how the

WILLIAM JENNINGS BRYAN
From his latest photograph by Townsend, Lincoln, Nebraska

THE HOME LIFE OF WILLIAM JENNINGS BRYAN

BY WILLIS J. ABBOT

⬧ THE DEMOCRATIC LEADER WITH HIS WIFE AND HIS CHIL-
DREN—THE FINE ESTATE AT FAIRVIEW, NEAR LINCOLN,
NEBRASKA, AND THE BUSY BUT CHEERFUL ROUTINE OF THE
HOUSEHOLD—A PICTURE OF SIMPLE AMERICAN DOMESTICITY

ONE must concede a certain humor-
ous side to any description of the
"home life" of a gentleman who, having just completed a tour of the world
occupying some eighteen months, remains
at home twenty-four hours and then
starts off on a political pilgrimage
through the Southern States by way of
rest from the rigors of foreign travel.
Few men in this country have traveled

Figure 1.4 *Human interest profile of the politician William Jennings Bryan, focusing on his 'home life' and marriage (1907)*

Figure 1.5 *Full-page Sunday supplement feature on Consuelo Vanderbilt, soon to become the Duchess of Marlborough, entirely devoted to personal details (1895)*

idea of the film star had to be *invented* and arose through the efforts of the fledgling film industry itself. In Reading 1.1, deCordova describes three stages that cumulatively created the film star. First, there was the invention of the very idea of *film* acting, that is, the idea that acting is something you do in a film. The second stage developed the idea that actors had names and could be recognised by the public from film to film. At the third stage, actors were given personalities by the studios, thus inaugurating the idea of the film star that we know today. The concept of the film star marked a new kind of knowledge about actors and was stitched together both from their films (together with the new conceptions of acting) *and* their private lives, as circulated in the press.

Figure 1.6 *Full-page photo essay accompanying a feature story on the actor Ethel Barrymore (1903)*

Reading 1.1 Activity

Now read the following extract from Richard deCordova 'The emergence of the star system in America'. You may find some of the terminology in Reading 1.1 a little difficult at first, so you may need to read it through more than once. Then make a note of your answers to the following questions:

- What was the importance of the 'picture personality'?
- What were the main differences between the 'picture personality' and the star?
- What does deCordova mean by 'intertextuality' and why is this important?

Reading 1.1

Richard deCordova, 'The emergence of the star system in America'

The emergence of the star system can perhaps best be seen as the emergence of a knowledge and analysed in these terms. Before 1909 virtually none of the players' names were known to the public, but by 1912 most of them had been 'discovered' (Slide, 1978). It is clear from this example that the 'picture personality' was the result of a particular production and circulation of knowledge. Studio publicity departments, films and fan magazines produced and promulgated this knowledge. In this paper I want to examine the rules by which this knowledge was produced and the various transformations these rules underwent.

The emergence of the star system involved a strict regulation of the type of knowledge produced about the actor. I will argue that the development of this system was effected through three significant transformations in this regard. These can be listed in the order of their appearance: (1) the discourse on acting, (2) the picture personality and (3) the star.

Before discussing these three stages individually, let me note that the appearance of the second, the picture personality, did not mean the disappearance of the first, the discourse on acting (or for that matter, the third the disappearance of the second). This transformation can best be characterized as a progressive overlaying of discourses and knowledges about a particular site – the actor.

The discourse on acting

Before 1907 there was no discourse on the film actor. Textual productivity was focused elsewhere, for the most part on the apparatus itself, on its magical abilities and its capacity to reproduce the real. It was obvious that people were represented on the screen, but the thought that these people were actors was very likely not considered. Acting was a profession of the legitimate stage, quite foreign to the milieu of the cinema's early development. The stage, after all, not only had actors, but also stars. The cinema's complete non-observance of these forms prior to 1907 is a testament to its relatively thoroughgoing disassociation from a theatrical model of representation.

[...]

Around 1907 another discourse began to supersede this discourse on the apparatus, one which included and eventually placed into the foreground the role of human labour in the production of film. This should [...] be viewed [...] as the regulated appearance of a certain kind of knowledge. This knowledge [...] resituate[d] the site of textual productivity for the spectator away from the work of the apparatus itself. [...] it was the actor/star that finally became central in this regard.

[...]

The emergence of what is called here the 'picture performer' depended on a knowledge of the performer's existence outside of the narrative of the film itself. [...]

[...]

The reader must confront the fictional status of that which is photographed by the camera. This attention to the fact that the scenes enacted in moving pictures were 'not real but feigned' had a direct bearing on the status of those who appeared in films; it worked to establish the filmed body as a site of fictional production. [...]

Such [accounts] refer to the reality *behind* that representation: that is, to the creative labour of those who appear in films [...]

The discourse on acting was fundamental to the institutionalisation of the cinema. [...] This [...] signalled a new form of product individuation more in keeping with an increasingly rationalised production system; the audience's appreciation would no longer be confined to the magic of the machine or the [...] thing photographed but would involve the possibility of discriminating – at the level of performance – between different films.

The picture personality

The picture personality was to be the principal site of product individualisation throughout the period. By 1909 picture personalities had begun to appear, either by their own names or by names the public assigned them. This is usually considered the beginning of the star system. It is indeed around this time that the star emerges as an economic reality. However, I have made a distinction between the picture personality and the star, assigning the emergence of the former to the year 1909 and the latter to 1914. There is a relation of knowledge specific to the picture personality which distinguishes it significantly from the star.

Three predominant forms of knowledge emerged to produce the picture personality. The first pertained to the circulation of the name. Through a dual movement of concealment and revelation the player's name was constituted as a site of knowledge. [...] In fact, there was an intense proliferation of knowledge about the picture personalities during this time [...]

Early fan magazines depended to a large extent on the pleasure the public took in knowing the players' names. Such features as *Motion Picture Story Magazine's* 'Popular Player Puzzle' appealed precisely to this. The following puzzle, for example, was proposed: 'A favourite pet of the children'. The answer was the actor John Bunny. [...]

What is at stake here is a type of identification in the most usual sense of the word: the identification of an actor in a specific film with a name. However, this identification extended well beyond the single film. What the name designated above all was a form of intertextuality, the recognition and identification of an actor from film to film.

This intertextuality emerged as a measure of the increasing regularity and regulation of the cinematic institution – both in its product (the same actors appeared regularly) and more crucially, in terms of its audience, which had to go to the cinema often for this intertextual meaning to arise. This intertextuality can be posited as the second form of knowledge which constituted the picture personality. This knowledge, however, was not produced solely in the cinema; journalistic discourse supported it as well. The most important point to make about this intertextuality is that it restricted knowledge about the players to the ... films they were in. The term 'picture personality' is itself evidence of this restriction. The site of interest was to be the personality of the player as it was depicted in film. [...]

A third type of knowledge that constituted the picture personality pertained to the professional experience of the actor. In so far as this knowledge related to the actor's previous film experience it worked to establish the intertextual space between films discussed earlier.

Figure 1.7 *The picture personality as a site of product individuation. The Orpheum Theatre, Oklahoma City, Oklahoma, 1912*

However this knowledge often referred to the actor's stage experience and can be seen as a continuation of the discourse on acting.

> The great success of Miss Lottie Briscoe is not surprising when it is remembered that she was, for years, with that master of dramatic art, Richard Mansfield. Miss Briscoe has already won a host of admirers in the motion picture world by her clever and her pleasing personality.
>
> The Motion Picture Story Magazine, 1911, p.23

[...] this discourse on acting worked to legitimise film through reference to the acting of the stage. It is important to note that this legitimation was effected entirely at the level of profession. The emergence of the picture personality did not signal any significant shift in this regard. One writer, attempting to explain why people were falling in love with matinee idols, concluded that it proved that the idol's 'acting, as well as their personality must be pretty much the same thing'(*Moving Picture World*, 1910, p.468). Knowledge about the picture personality was restricted to the player's professional existence – either his/her representation in films or to his/her previous work in film and theatre.

The star

It is along these lines that one can distinguish the star from the picture personality. [...] With the emergence of the star, the question of the player's existence outside his/her work in films entered discourse.

This question entailed a significant transformation in the regulation of knowledge concerning the player. The manufacturers would no longer be able to restrict knowledge about the players to the textuality of the films they were in. Thus, the absolute control the studios had over the picture personality's image was, in one sense, relinquished, but only so that it could be extended to another sphere. The private lives of the stars emerged as a new site of knowledge and truth.

In 1914 a short story appeared in *Photoplay* entitled 'Loree Starr – Photoplay Idol' (Robert Kerr, 1914). It is most remarkable for its subtitle – 'A Fascinating Serial Story Presenting a New Type of Hero'. This new hero is precisely the star as distinguished from the picture personality. It is around this time that the star becomes the subject of a narrative which is quite separate from his/her work in any particular film.

Here is a quote from 1916 which quite explicitly poses the question of the star: 'And even in these days of the all-seeing camera-eye there are scores of heroic deeds, of patently self-sacrificing acts, performed by the film folk which never reach pictures or print (*The Motion Picture Classic*, 1916, p.55). It ends by asking – 'Is your REEL hero ever a REAL hero?'

So, private and professional become two autonomous spheres that can be articulated in paradigm. It is important to note however, that these two spheres are constituted in what might be called an analogous or redundant relation. The real hero behaves just like the reel hero. The private life of the star was not to be in contradiction with his/her film image – at least not in terms of its moral tenor.1 The power of the cinema was thus augmented by the extension of its textual and ideological functioning into the discourse on the star. [...]

[NB: The argument in this extract is developed more fully in *Picture Personalities: The Emergence of the Star System in America* by Richard deCordova (1990).]

References

Kerr, R. (1914) 'Loree Starr – Photoplay Idol', *Photoplay*, September.

Moving Picture World (1910) vol.6, no.12, p.468.

Slide, A. (1978) *Aspects of American Film History Prior to 1920*, Metuchen, NJ, Scarecrow Press.

The Motion Picture Classic (1916) February, p.55.

The Motion Picture Story Magazine (1911) February, vol.1, no.1 p.23.

Note

1 Some precision is necessary here. A certain level of contradiction was absolutely essential to the presentation of performance during the period. The force of Mary Pickford's performance in *Stella Maris* (1918), for instance, is dependent upon the discrepancy between Pickford's identity as a wealthy movie star and her appearance in the film (in one of two roles) as a penniless orphan. My argument here is that this field of contradiction did not generally engage moral categories.

Reading source

deCordova, 1991, pp.19–27 ■ ■ ■

According to deCordova, the development of picture personalities was *the* crucial step in the emergence of the concept of the film star, although it built on the earlier idea that film involved an actor or 'performer'. You may have noted deCordova's emphasis on 'knowledge' – he describes the star system as 'the emergence of a knowledge' and says that, over the three stages, the type of knowledge produced about film actors was regulated by the industry. In emphasising the idea of knowledge deCordova indicates that stars did not evolve naturally along with the film industry; they were not just part of a general cultural Zeitgeist (see Section 1). Rather, they had to be *invented*, in this case within one particular institutional context, and through the creation of specific kinds of information, skills and beliefs – about what acting meant, what audiences should know about those who appeared in films and the skills they displayed, and so on. Thus, the picture personality was based on cinema-goers' knowledge of the name of the performer behind the performance. This was achieved 'intertextually', a term that deCordova uses to stress the relationship between individual texts, or films in this case. He means that cinema audiences came to recognise actors' faces and names *across* a number of films as a result of becoming regular cinema-goers. However, at this picture personality stage, knowledge of film personalities was restricted to their professional practice – the film characters they played. There was no discourse about actors' personalities outside the film roles they played. In contrast, the post-1919 stars were built on public personalities that literally had lives of their own outside the text of the films they starred in. Thus, the definition of the film star persona depended on the idea that we could know something about those lives. These stars were the subjects of discourses about their private lives and intimate relationships. There were other important textual and technological devices, not referred to in Reading 1.1, which also contributed to the discourse of the picture personality and then the film star. Of most significance was the close-up, first invented in the D.W. Griffith film, *For Love of Gold* (USA, dir. Griffith, 1908). The close-up cemented the impression of intimacy with the performer behind the role s/he played because it allowed a close view of the actor's face. The spectator's attention was drawn away from the role being played to the actor's face and 'looks' (Schickel, 1985, p.34; Dyer, 1979).

One important aspect of deCordova's work is the method he uses. This is a close examination of the language used in the actual statements that circulated within the film industry, its publicity departments and in the texts of film and popular journalism of the time. The development of a particular medium should, deCordova implies, be approached as contingent on historical context. We should not assume in advance of looking at the historical context that there are inevitable continuities between different media. As we have seen, the popular press were, even before the use of half-tone (photographic) prints, creating celebrity 'personalities' from actors, nobility and politicians. Moreover, vaudeville and theatrical stars were well established in the last decades of the nineteenth century. However, for the reasons deCordova gives, it was only when a number of discourses within the film industry came together that it became possible to refer to a type of person called a film star, who could be named, recognised and treated in the same manner as established theatrical stars. The broader lesson we can take from deCordova's historical approach brings us back to the points about change and continuity raised in Section 1. That is, it is by looking at the small details of history, at how things are actually described and understood in their own historical time, that we observe the nuances of change. In paying attention to these nuances we find that change is piecemeal rather than total, and therefore involves elements of discontinuity as well as continuity with the past.

3.3 Celebrity persona in the early twentieth century

By the 1920s, celebrity journalism in the US had become ubiquitous. One statistic is quite striking: by 1930, Hollywood was the third largest news source in the USA (Balio, 1985, p.266). However, deCordova notes at the end of Reading 1.1 that at the inception of the film star, 'the private life of the star was not to be in contradiction with his/her film image – at least not in terms of its moral tenor'. However, things had changed by the late 1920s. Joan Crawford wrote to her readers in a 1928 issue of

Photoplay that she had not told her life story because 'I was afraid to tell it to you. You have one idea of Joan Crawford, now you are going to have another' (quoted in Gamson, 1992, p.21). *Photoplay*, a fan magazine, carried a gossip column entitled 'Facts and near-facts about the great and near-great of film land' (Schickel, 1985, p.38), as well as confessional stories by stars themselves. This suggests that the mediated persona of stars had become over this short space of time even less dependent on the professional film character and more bound up with the idea of the 'real', authentic life of the human person behind the professional role.

Activity 1.4

Think about what you have read so far in this section and spend a few minutes making some notes to answer the following questions:

- What are the key points about the history of celebrity that can inform our understanding of celebrity today?

- To what extent do you think that today's concept of celebrity is similar to its predecessors of a hundred years or so ago? ■ ■ ■

The examples cited in this section indicate how, by the early decades of the twentieth century, the means of attaining public visibility was mediated in a particular way, that is, by an industrialised production of media (see Book Introduction). It was subject to the techniques of mass reproduction and to the widespread availability of mediations based on recording technologies. In many ways, therefore, some key elements of celebrity culture that we are familiar with today were becoming commonplace. First, entertainment values and film's star system merged with news reportage. Second, distinctions between public and private lives were softened and revelations about the latter became central to celebrity persona from the early part of the twentieth century, although importantly, as deCordova shows, this was uneven, and occurred much later in the film industry. Stories about stars' lives that had little connection with their professional work began to frequent the popular press.

There have been long-term consequences of making private life part of a celebrity's persona. For example, celebrities themselves have attempted to use their economic power, via agents and publicists, to control their personae via litigation. Consequently, as recognised in a number of recent cases, judges have had to consider what may be deemed 'harm' to a celebrity when their privacy is intruded upon (via 'snatched' paparazzi photographs). This leads to complex and difficult judgements when, paradoxically, the very same celebrities deliberately court publicity so as to maintain a consistent and marketable persona (see Schilling, 2003; Milmo, 2003).

4   Politics in celebrity culture today

In the previous section we saw how some of the characteristics of
celebrity construction that we may be familiar with today were first
established some time ago. To some extent, then, celebrity may not be an
entirely new phenomenon – it has developed in a gradual and uneven
fashion. Let us now turn to the present day and consider the relationship
between celebritisation and political life. To what extent have the mass
media celebritised politics? Are the concerns about celebrity culture by
the cultural decline critics (outlined in Section 1) justified: is there
evidence that mass-mediated celebrity has had more troubling effects on
our culture than is allowed by the positive, populist perspective?

At the very least, populists regard celebrity culture as harmless
entertainment and do not think it affects more important social and
political processes and events. But, as we have seen in Section 1.1, many
populists go further to argue that celebrity gives voice to those who
historically have been unseen and unheard. A rather different view, held
by the cultural decline theorists, is that saturation coverage of celebrity in
the media is systematically distorting how politics is conducted and
altering, for the worse, the relationship between citizens and their
governments (see Corner and Pels, 2003). They are concerned, for
example, that celebrities, essentially part of a commercial entertainment
sector, have begun to degrade the more sober arena of political affairs.
This section studies the claims that there are new ways in which
contemporary celebrity-oriented media interact with political life. To a
great extent, as you will see, this means an assessment of the nature of
celebrity power. That is, not simply the power of individual celebrities,
but the power of the *system* of celebrity, which includes, for example, the
institutionalisation of public relations as part of the media and the
technical devices of close-up telephoto lenses.

4.1   Celebrities and power

What is the relationship between celebrities and power? Or, to put it
another way, in what ways can celebrities be construed as having an effect
on politics? In mediated representations, celebrities – from pop and film
stars to sports stars – are often seen mingling with politicians, as we noted
in Section 1. However, according to one of the earliest writers to address
this issue, Francesco Alberoni (1972) (also see Dyer, 1979), there is an
important distinction between these types of celebrities and other public
figures such as politicians whose 'fame' is a by-product of their public role.
Stars are an elite, but a 'powerless elite'. That is, they are a group of
people whose institutional power is very weak or non-existent. For
Alberoni, there are some basic conditions for this distinction. It
presupposes a modern democracy that is based on authority rather than

personal power. Alberoni wanted to account for the ways in which the social order is legitimated other than by sheer force. In an important sense, George Bush and Tony Blair, unlike Louis XIV or Elizabeth I, do not wield *personal* power of the charismatic type that we saw Weber describing earlier (see Section 2.1), though they may also be charismatic (for further discussion of this, see Chapter 4). For what they can or cannot do is constrained by various legislative and judicial procedures. They are in the *role* of governing, in-between elections, on the basis of a legitimacy and authority that comes from those elections. Alberoni also stressed the existence of a structured social system in which there are demarcated spheres of interest and values. These have clear boundaries between them. Celebrities and politicians exist in different spheres; their success and credibility are judged according to different criteria and they are rewarded in different ways. So, there is not – *or should not be* – any 'danger' of the charisma of celebrities becoming important from a political point of view, even though they may be part of an elite group in their own social sector.

However, Alberoni did not account for the fact that although a celebrity may not be directly a political player, s/he may still have political or ideological significance. First, the media often use celebrities or celebritise individuals in order to convey a preferred political stance, even though this is often indirect. McVeigh (see Section 1.1) may not have wielded institutional power as do politicians, but arguably his persona was put to powerful use in the battle of mediated ideas to persuade media audiences of the truth of certain definitions of terrorism. This might be considered highly political at a time when terrorist acts are, and seem likely to continue to be, associated with those who are not American. Second, the line between politicians themselves and celebrity may indeed be blurred. According to Marshall (1997) there is now a 'convergence in the source of power between the political leader and other forms of celebrity' (p.19). For example, established celebrities do become politicians: in recent history one only has to think of Ronald Reagan, former President of the US, and Arnold Schwarzenegger, who based his campaign for Governor of California (in large part) on his celebrity charisma. There are also developments of a more systematic nature, such as the steady growth in the number of entertainers seeking public office and gaining political power in countries such as the Philippines. Not only was ex-President Joseph Estrada a former action film star, but according to some there is a new power elite in the country that has been characterised as a 'celebritocracy'. In the Phillipines Senate, close to a third of the sitting senators launched their political careers by way of television, film and show business (see Celdran, 2001).

The discussion of individual celebrities and the power they wield, however, fails to address how celebritisation has worked more systematically to alter the domain of politics, something that has preoccupied media theorists such as John Corner and Dirk Pels (2003). They suggest that domains of endeavour (such as the mass media and political processes, or entertainment and news journalism), which may once have been separate in terms of their values and practices, are now becoming even more entwined (see Section 1). As we saw in Section 3, press journalism, even in the early twentieth century, was increasingly given over to entertainment-based and celebrity coverage. With the expansion of the media and commercial entertainment industries, we might therefore expect that celebrity is increasingly used by the media to make sense of political and social affairs (see Corner and Pels, 2003).

Let us now turn to the case of one campaign organisation, the British charity Oxfam, which uses entertainment celebrities to attract publicity. In reading through the next section your aim is to assess whether you think this fusion of celebrity coverage and social campaigning is a positive or a worrying trend. Does it mean that political debate is made more accessible, or is it part of a cultural decline, a tendency towards trivialisation?

4.2 Oxfam's celebrities: politics as entertainment?

Oxfam is one of a number of international development charities that has recently developed a policy of using celebrities as a way of getting its campaigns widely known and increasing its media coverage (see Cunningham, 2002). Oxfam, like many other charities, has someone called a 'celebrity co-ordinator' dedicated to the task. Oxfam targets a range of media and selects a celebrity based on its analysis of which media market, and therefore which segment of the public, it wants to reach. We will concentrate on the category of 'long-haul' celebrities who have a long-term association with Oxfam and who are taken abroad to create a media event every 18 months or so. Whenever they are the focus of a media story they 'hook' a mention for Oxfam. We focus here on two of their most popular celebrities, Michelle Collins, ex-*East Enders* star, and Claire Goose, a television star formerly in *Waking the Dead*. Collins and Goose attract coverage in the popular market – from mass circulation tabloids such as *The Sun* and *The Mirror*, to *Hello!* and *OK!* celebrity magazines, *Woman's Own* magazine and GMTV (ITV).

Activity 1.5

Look at Figures 1.8 and 1.9, and Plates 11a and 11b in the colour section.

For each picture, note down what you notice about the role the featured celebrity is playing in relation to Oxfam. How are foreign events and politics being represented? Do not bother trying to read the text of the article unless you want to, simply look at the layout. ■ ■ ■

★ PEOPLE SPECIAL ★ PEOPLE SPECIAL ★ PEOPLE SPECIAL ★

ANGEL MICHELLE

MICHELLE Collins admits that during her EastEnders days, the role of Oxfam ambassador was one she would not have been offered. "I wouldn't have been asked," she says laughing. "Cindy was a vamp, who tried to kill her husband. She didn't exactly have a caring, kind image, did she?"

But now, established as one of our leading TV actresses, she is seen as a far more suitable role model. Both on and off screen, the 36-year-old mum has matured and bloomed with confidence since leaving Albert Square behind.

"I think people take me more seriously now. I think I take myself more seriously with the work I have done. I've been in programmes that have centred around me so people must think I am responsible."

She adds: "I have matured and grown up a bit. Being a mother changed me. Hopefully I'm a better person now and a better actress."

As spokesperson for Oxfam's Education Now! Campaign, Michelle travelled to Brazil earlier in the year to visit projects and meet street children. With a young daughter of her own, the scenes clearly moved her. "There were times when I felt I couldn't cope. I wanted to cry but I stopped myself because I hate it when people cry on those documentaries."

She describes kids as young as five-addicted to glue-sniffing and girls who suffered

The actress renowned for playing one of the toughest vixens in soap history is revealing her softer side as ambassador for Oxfam

BY MELANIE CLARKSON

multiple rapes. "It's just heartbreaking," she continues. "There were a couple of moments when I felt I couldn't cope. One day we visited this shanty town. It was the most horrible, horrible place where this woman lived. She didn't get running water or anything. She had a son who was a drug addict and a daughter who'd run away and was a prostitute.

The only time she ever came home was to steal from her mum. She said the next time I see my daughter she will be in a coffin. As a mother myself, that was just terrible."

Far less starry than you imagine, Michelle has impressed Oxfam campaigners with the vigour with which she has approached this new role. Admitting that she hates to back down until she has succeeded, she

is currently organising a fashion event to raise funds for the charity and will visit Manchester's Cornerhouse Cinema on April 13 to talk about the plight of the children she met.

As well as this charity role, the blonde actress is in the middle of filming a new Christmas thriller for the BBC. A further series of Daylight Robbery awaits after that. Although she says she thought she would never work again after EastEnders, she is one of that rare breed who has flourished, finding a niche playing strong but vulnerable thirtysomething woman.

"I can't believe how well it has gone," she says breathily. "I don't know why me. I'm just one of the lucky ones, I suppose. It's been two years now since I have left and it's still getting better."

While she still wants to do "a bit more good telly" films are also beckoning. She's been up for a few parts but claims: "There is still such a snobbery within the film industry about people who are known for their work on TV. But it is getting better with people like Ray Winstone and Kathy Burke."

She adds: "If I don't get offered the right role, I might just create my own project. I'd like to do a domestic drama, something people can relate to," she explains before adding. "Anything with a strong, female lead."

■ Michelle Collins will attend a special screening of the Oscar-nominated Brazilian film Central Station at the Cornerhouse Cinema on Thursday. Call the box office on 0161 2001500.

Figure 1.8 Michelle Collins, actor and Oxfam ambassador

MICHELLE COLLINS IN BRAZIL

United Nations promise of worldwide primary education for all by 2015 because, so far, targets are not being met.

"Education is the single most important weapon against poverty," says Michelle. "It saves lives and gives people a voice. But, worldwide, 125 million children do not get an education."

In Brazil, 30 per cent of children miss out on at least some of their primary schooling. Michelle talked with many of those children failed by the system – and with others now being helped by projects supported by Oxfam, including a centre for young abused girls and a detox centre for street children addicted to glue-sniffing.

For Michelle, the trip had to be fitted into a frantic work schedule. Since leaving *East-Enders* she has reinvented herself from soap star to versatile actress, with three hit TV series – *Real Women, Daylight Robbery* and *Sunburn* – behind her, and a list of up-coming projects as long as your arm. She is starring in new ITV sitcom *Up Rising* alongside *Dad* star Kevin McNally, Anton Rodgers and Nicola Pagett. And next in line come two thrillers to be shown at Christmas, another series of *Daylight Robbery* and a ▶ drama series, shooting

Figure 1.9 Michelle Collins in Brazil in a page spread from Hello! *magazine*

We can make a number of observations about the textual devices used by these spreads. You may have immediately noticed how central the *celebrity* is, in both the words and pictures (Figures 1.8 and 1.9 and Plates 11a and 11b). In the pictures, the focus is always on them, their reactions, their facial expressions and their 'look'. Some spreads focus solely on the (youthful and feminine aspects of the) celebrity and imitate the glamorous style of a fashion shoot. The features merge information about the celebrity's private life (Claire Goose is 'ending her four year old relationship with fellow Casualty actor ...') with their career aspirations and their reactions to the country they are visiting. In fact, the sub-heading in Figure 1.8 confuses the real person with her fictional role: 'The actor renowned for playing one of the toughest vixens in soap history is revealing her softer side as ambassador for Oxfam'. What dominates these spreads is the compelling drama of the celebrity's life and career – they are a conduit through which readers come to understand the politics of development. The feelings of the celebrities and their responses to what they see are uppermost in importance; Goose writes a personal diary for *Hello!* There is an emphasis on their own experiences of hardship or distress, providing them with a link – though tenuous – with the suffering and hardship of those they are visiting. You may have also noticed an ethnic dimension here – each celebrity is white, individualised and named, whereas the black nationals tend to be grouped and represented as an anonymous 'background'. This affects the way we identify with the pictures and stories – it is more likely that readers will relate to those who are named and individualised and effectively made the *topic* of the story, that is, the celebrities themselves.

Oxfam says that since their campaigns inevitably involve very complex economic and political arguments, the function of celebrity is to convert these into digestible and easily understandable chunks of information that will fit into the contexts of media viewing (such as snatching a read of *Hello!* on your lunch-time break). Oxfam's celebrity co-ordinator identifies the charity's predicament: they must compete for media coverage in a context where '... if a celebrity talks to a girl who has seen her mother shot and comes out and cries, you cry with her. Issues on their own do not mean very much and newspapers will never be interested in them' (Clare Lewis, in Evans, 2003). Oxfam's aim is to cement the connection between the charity and the celebrity they work with; in effect the celebrity becomes a branding device.

As you can see from this example, one central function of the dissemination of celebrities in a political context is to make a highly complex, and sometimes rather opaque, world simpler by furnishing it with a 'human' or personalised dimension (see Smith, 2002). Through personalising an event and showing their ordinary but conspicuous compassion, celebrities supply audiences with a point of identification with what is often a politically tangled situation. Oxfam make the judgement that they are in a position where they have little choice and take the view that it is better to turn dominant media values to your advantage. A populist view would be more positive, arguing that this kind of personalisation of the political and the development of the 'soundbite' will have the effect of bringing foreign affairs issues to ordinary people's — *we th* attention in a way that is accessible to them (Fiske, 1992; Street, 2001). The alternative is to risk losing all media coverage through the adoption of a more purist, cultural decline position, which would emphasise that the complexity and difficulty of trade and development issues is simply sidelined and watered down by the banalities of celebrity lifestyles (see the discussion in Smith, 2002). You may think, were you to take this position, that these images speak volumes for the rather uncomfortable way in which the aesthetic and entertainment pleasures that are historically part of the meaning of celebrity can suppress the political and economic issues at stake (see Franklin, 1994; see the discussion in Chapter 2, Section 5). Given the way the stories are presented and the textual devices used, you might feel that readers are more likely to be fascinated by Michelle Collins' life story, emotional dilemmas and choice of fashion, rather than the political detail of Brazilian trade relations. Whatever view you hold, the case of Oxfam indicates how the use of celebrities has now gone far beyond that of consumer product promotion, and how celebrity culture and current affairs coverage have merged. At the same time, these techniques do have precedents. It is now twenty years since the globally televised 'telethon', Live Aid, led by Bob Geldof and other leading pop stars of the time.

Moving onto the world of formal politics, writers such as Pels (2003) argue that celebritisation of the kind we have seen in the Oxfam example has had the effect of re-fashioning politics by turning it into an aesthetic or at least stylistic exercise: appearance and presentation matters more than substance. Marketing techniques and the minutiae of visual and verbal presentation — such as dress codes and voice training — are used to turn politicians into distinctive personalities, and are regarded as essential indicators of a political stance (Pels, 2003, p.61). The ways in which politicians perform in the media, including their physical characteristics, are now key criteria for promotion within government ranks (Corner, 2003). 'Personalities' have to a great extent, it is claimed, become the framework around which political positions are 'recognised' or through which attachments are made to parties or factions of them, much as Michelle Collins is a way of branding Oxfam. Politicians trade on their ordinariness rather than their distance from the population; at the same time the media use personal information about politicians' lives to assess their public standing. In this way their political stance is seen to rest on their personal credibility, which means we are asked to judge politicians on the basis of private, moral preferences. So, we get to know, because it *appears* to have relevance for their credibility in the public sphere, which football team a politician supports, who they are having an affair with, what schools their children go to, whether they have had a controversial vaccine, and so on.

So far we have referred to the *content* of mass media coverage, the way it has brought together the domains and values of celebrity and politics. But, do the *techniques* the media use encourage a celebritisation process and in so doing do they alter the conduct and meaning of political life? In the next and final section we look more closely at the techniques of media communication, at the development of new media technologies such as telephoto lenses, radio and television, to assess the extent to which they have altered the representation and conduct of political life.

4.3 The celebritisation of politics and the politics of celebritisation

As we saw in the Book Introduction, mass media communications are largely one-way, reaching a diffuse population. They are also, in the words of John Thompson (1995, p.84), 'quasi-interactive', meaning that individuals separated in space and often time are linked together in a process of symbolic exchange even when this is not reciprocal. This *impression* of reciprocity is termed 'para-social interaction' by two media theorists, Donald Horton and Richard Wohl (1993), in an important and much cited article written in 1956. They were concerned with the relationships that are formed between people who experience each other only through the mass media. What is specific to the new post-print mass media, and by this they mean radio, television and film, is that these offer the *illusion* of face-to-face interaction with the performer, whether these be fictional characters, political figures or 'personalities' and performers.

Broadcast media personnel are trained to speak to the camera as if it was a personal friend, an imitation of a face-to-face encounter. You may have noticed a news presenter or chat-show host saying, direct to camera, that they will 'see you tomorrow'. You may agree that this is less a factual statement (they will not actually see you at all, even less do they know you) than a rhetorical one! This 'as if' quality hides the fact that there is no actual reciprocity and that the interaction is entirely controlled by the performers and mediated by the larger apparatus of television or radio production. US media theorist Joshua Meyrowitz, in an important book called *No Sense of Place* (1985), develops the insights in Horton and Wohl's article. He suggests that those such as performers or politicians who appear in the media often find themselves exploiting the familiarity of the para-social interaction: 'The para-social framework may explain why many singing stars turn to more and more personal lyrics and themes as their careers develop and why public officials often add more private information to their public speeches as they become more widely known' (1985, p.119).

Meyrowitz argues that politicians under conditions of para-social media lose their aura of greatness and distance. The 24-hour flow of information has essentially undermined their elevated, unobtainable status. As you saw in the article on the democrat politician Jennings Bryan (see Figure 1.4), this is not entirely new; the media was already by 1900 eroding the barriers between politicians' traditional 'back' (private) and 'front' (public) regions. However, the difference between now and then is that leaders up to the 1960s were able to control access to themselves. For example, as recently as the beginning of the 1950s, during Eisenhower's presidency, a system of informal rules meant that the press was not allowed to quote the President directly without permission, and certainly before the 1920s most people had never heard the voice of a Prime Minister (Meyrowitz, 1985, p.168). However, recording, and now electronic, technology and such devices as the telephoto lens, says Meyrowitz, minimises the distance between audience and performer revealing much that is intended and unintended in the performance of a politician (see Figure 1.10). It is perhaps not surprising that given these conditions, politicians regard the public as a media audience who must be mollified or pleased, talked to rather than talked with (see Whillock, 1999, p.7).

Meyrowitz (1985) also stresses the dependency of the print media on electronic media: the press often describes events in a manner 'which simulates what one might have seen and heard on television' (p.178). The inclusion of conversational tics such as 'um' and 'you know' in quotations is one example, but more importantly he notes the reporting of aural and visual phenomena in the press that might have gone unnoticed to most people at the actual event: 'The sweat on a politician's brow, a tear running down a face, or a nervous twitch may become part of the print description — because the "event" is now defined in terms of how it appeared on television' (Meyrowitz, p.178) (Figure 1.10).

Meyrowitz describes how the intense staging of the political as para-social intimacy, especially in an age of electronic media, has an effect on the relationship between those who are represented and those who are representatives in a democracy (see also Pels, 2003). Where there was distance, we now have apparent closeness (see Sennett, 1977) because of continuous media exposure that makes politics seem less formal and politicians more ordinary. The general sense of the openness of situations that has resulted from the widespread dissemination of electronic media is just one aspect of a more general suspicion of closed systems (Meyrowitz, 1985, p.183), manifested in closed meetings, secret ballots

HUTTON REPORT: THE AFTERMATH

THE INDEPENDENT
Thursday 5 February 2004

Tony Blair leaving the House of Commons yesterday after being heckled by protesters from the public gallery during the Hutton debate   *Gretel Ensignia*

Blair admits he did not know 45-minute claim referred to battlefield weapons

BY NIGEL MORRIS AND BEN RUSSELL

TONY BLAIR admitted yesterday that he led the crucial parliamentary debate which approved the war in Iraq without knowing the full truth behind the Government's claim that Iraq could deploy weapons of mass destruction within 45 minutes.

He was pressed in the Commons to spell out when he knew that the claim Iraq could launch a deadly attack with weapons of mass destruction within that period related only to battlefield missiles. Mr Blair said: "I've already indicated exactly when this came to my attention; it wasn't before the debate on 18 March. "When you say that a battlefield weapon would not be a weapon of mass destruction, if there were chemical or biological or nuclear battlefield weapons that most certainly would be held as a weapon of mass destruction and the idea that their use wouldn't threaten regional stability I find somewhat eccentric."

In comments that appeared to contradict evidence to the Hutton inquiry by Geoff Hoon, the Defence Secretary, Mr Blair admitted: "The report from the Secret Intelligence Service did not specify the specific delivery system to which the time of 45 minutes applied."

Critics of the war seized on Mr Blair's comments. **Robin Cook**, the former foreign secretary, told MPs: "I find it difficult to reconcile what I knew and what I'm sure the Prime Minister knew at the time we had the vote in March."

The claim by Dr Brian Jones in *The Independent* yesterday that the anxieties of intelligence officers about the dossier were overruled was repeatedly aired in a fractious debate on the Hutton report that had to be briefly suspended because of heckling by anti-war demonstrators.

Mr Blair acknowledged that there was a question over the failure of intelligence chiefs to consider the doubts of Dr Jones over the threat posed by Iraq. But the Prime Minister insisted that questions of procedure within Dr Jones's department were "a million miles away" from the former BBC reporter Andrew Gilligan's claim that Downing Street "sexed up" the dossier that made the case for war. He said that Dr Jones' concern about the wording was "hardly of earth-shattering significance". Mr Blair said: "Those concerns never came to the full Joint Intelligence Committee, let alone Downing Street. ... The fact is that what you cannot possibly say is that Downing Street had anything to do with this. "There may well be issues that arise in relation to, for example, what are procedures within the department and so on, but that is a million miles away from the allegation that was broadcast."

Mr Blair rejected demands, led by the Tory leader, **Michael Howard**, to publish the secret intelligence that is said to have backed the 45-minute claim. He said: "Dr Jones saw all the intelligence there was to see on it; so incidentally did Lord Hutton. The intelligence referred to in the [*Independent*] article which he did not see was, I am told, intelligence about the production of chemical and biological warfare agents.

"He did not see it because the SIS [Secret Intelligence Services] put it out on a very restricted basis due to source sensitivity. His superiors were, however, briefed on the intelligence. It does not actually bear on the 45-minute point at all."

Mr Blair argued that the BBC report which prompted the Hutton inquiry was "100 per cent wrong", but he conceded that intelligence service concerns over the dossier's phrasing of the Government's dossier was the "grain of truth" behind Mr Gilligan's story.

Flanked by the Defence Secretary, Geoff Hoon, and 10 other cabinet ministers, Mr Blair agreed with one MP that opposition to the Hutton report's findings were sparked by "frustration" that no ministers had been forced out by the issue. He said: "The report itself – clear, forensic and utterly comprehensive in terms of the analysis of the evidence – is the best defence to the charges of government whitewash, often by the same people who just over a week ago were describing Lord Hutton as a model of impartiality, wisdom and insight."

Mr Howard urged Mr Blair to publish the original intelligence used to support the 45-minute claim. He said: "There are some things which can and should be done in relation to these issues, though which don't need the report of that inquiry; some things which can be done now.

"Writing in *The Independent* today, Dr Brian Jones has made a specific request to the Prime Minister to publish now the intelligence which he was not shown at the time ,which he says lies behind the Government's claims that Iraq was actively producing chemical weapons and could launch an attack within 45 minutes of an order to do so. Dr Jones clearly does not believe, given that Saddam Hussein has now been overthrown, that even if that intelligence came from a source that was sensitive then at the time when Saddam still ruled Iraq, it is sensitive now. It seems to me the request which Dr Jones has made is an entirely reasonable one."

Mr Howard told MPs that he had rejected the original terms of reference for the new inquiry because the committee "should consider the way in which the Government used the intelligence with which it had been provided".

Charles Kennedy, the Liberal Democrat leader, said: "The Government made every conceivable effort to have a public presentation, in terms of the interpretation of that document, that clearly was designed to move people decidedly in one direction, and one direction only. That is why so many of these questions remained outstanding then and remain outstanding now." **Andrew Mackinlay**, the Labour MP who described Dr Kelly as "chaff" during the scientist's appearance before the Foreign Affairs Committee, urged parliamentary committees not to take the "soft option".

He said: "It's our duty not to buckle under this. It seems to me that what we want are MPs who are still prepared to ignore the sign which says, 'no trespass, don't go here'. Where the door says, 'do not enter' you open it and go through and that's going to be my commitment to this House regardless of what has happened in the past, which I deeply regret."

Bernard Jenkin, shadow Defence Secretary at the time of the war, said: "If we want the public to believe that published intelligence information is intelligence and not propaganda we've got to be able to answer the question: at what stage does intelligence become propaganda when it is in the hands of the spin doctors and the politicians?"

Figure 1.10 An article in The Independent in 2004. The caption reads: 'Tony Blair leaving the House of Commons yesterday after being heckled by protesters from the public gallery during the Hutton debate'. Note how the image, supported by caption and headline, creates the impression of a man under pressure

and civil servants who claim allegiance to their ministers rather than speaking 'directly' to the electorate. Indeed, the first two administrations of the Blair government have probably been the first to systematically bypass the House of Commons and speak 'directly' to the 'public', by which is meant the media, on issues of the day (see Whillock, 1999).

Activity 1.6

Pause for a minute and think about what you have read so far in Section 4 about media content and media techniques. Make notes on the following:

- Do you think celebritisation has an impact on politics today in a way that is different from previous periods?
- To what extent do you think this has to do with the mass media?
- Do you think this is generally a positive development, as populists would argue, or does it provide you with cause for concern, like the cultural decline theorists? ■ ■ ■

There is much to be said for Meyrowitz's approach to these questions, for he pays attention to the specific technical devices used by the media that alter the terms and conditions under which politics and politicians operate. He and others present their analysis in dispassionate terms, but nonetheless point to trends that are also of considerable concern to those who take a more negative, cultural decline view (see Beniger, 1987; Hart, 1994; Franklin, 1994, 1998; Postman, 1985). However, we will reach a deeper understanding of the novelty of our own times if we are careful about what it is we are saying has changed. At this point, it is useful to return to some of the issues discussed earlier in the chapter about continuity and change.

Some who challenge Meyrowitz's account pointed out that the celebritisation of politics and the turning of politics into a public spectacle is not the consequence of the relatively recent medium of television, (see Briggs and Burke, 2002; Burke 1992). As you saw in Section 3, the public dramatisation and personalisation of politics was well established in Louis XIV's day (see Burke, 1992). Neither public relations nor the use of pseudo-events are unique to the period of the mass media, Peter Burke points out (1992). As he says, when it comes to the personalisation of politics, the similarities between the time of Louis XIV and our own period are striking. It should remind us 'not only of the importance of ritual, myth and symbol in politics at all times, but also of the continuity of particular myths and symbols in western societies' (1992, p.200). Nonetheless, in some important respects, the ways in which media interacts with modern politics does differ from 300 years ago. The first difference is the rise of legitimation by popular election.

Louis XIV represented God; today's governments represent the popular will of the nation's citizens, and therefore the art of persuasion is doubly important. Louis had to be presented as someone special, but he did not need to cultivate voters (Burke, 1992). His physical person was fused with his public role, as were Napoleon, Lenin and Stalin later on (Burke, 1992, p.205; Celdran, 2001). Second, the high social status of politicians no longer guarantees control of information about them (Meyrowitz, 1985). Politicians are now always 'on the job' and so there is increasingly less discontinuity between their public and their private lives: they are watched on holiday via telephoto lenses like any other celebrity. They present their own political predicaments as if they were grappling with difficult personal issues.

It can be argued, then, that what is new in recent years is that the power to represent politics and government has shifted from political leaders to the media. According to one commentator, 'the media have come to create and constitute the space in which politics now chiefly happens for most people in so-called "advanced societies" '(Castells, quoted in Blumler and Gurevitch, 2000, p.166). One effect of this shift, as has already been pointed out, is that politics is infused by the values and interests of media organisations themselves. Accordingly, powerful sets of values that are historically bound up with celebrity, such as intimacy, confession and revelation of personal lives, are 'leaked' into political life more generally. In this way politicians are vulnerable to the *personalisation* of politics and its effects. This personalisation of politics is another aspect of the celebritisation process that we introduced in our discussion of Timothy McVeigh.

For populists, these are positive developments because a more media-driven form of communication can respond more quickly to popular demand and can bypass 'faceless' government bureaucracies and the political elite. Populists might say that with celebritisation, the ordinary, more domestic, perhaps even female-friendly, way of looking at the world that the vast majority of media consumers can identify with, is at last at centre stage (see Lumby, 1999; Hartley, 1996, and for further discussion see Chapter 2).

In contrast, a cultural decline critic may point out that this shift of power to the media in general is dangerous because media organisations are largely in the hands of private corporations, have commercial gains to appeal to lowest common denominator values, are unelected and generally unaccountable. They argue that the emphasis on image management and branding in politics, and the focus on personal charisma drowns out political ideas and debate. They regard the professionalisation of political communication as a worrying manifestation of the media's increased role in public life. Political parties, at least, for example, in the UK and the US, become 'market-oriented organisations ... geared to the needs of virtually permanent campaigning' (Webb, quoted in Scammell, 2003). Communication between different political candidates and between politicians and the electorate is replaced by media personalities, pundits and pollsters who have an interest in camera-ready 'pseudo-events' and creating ritualistic conflicts between public figures (Pels, 2003, pp.46–7). When personality becomes enlarged in public life, they argue, some real dangers may ensue. As media theorist Pels warns:

> The star-struck individual or group easily forgets about the virtuality and asymmetry of the relationship in order to feel 'at one' with the political hero, while the hero may in turn delude himself into thinking that he immediately coincides with his following.
>
> Pels, 2003, p.60

Here, Pels neatly sums up something of the less conscious aspects of the dynamic between celebrities and their audiences to which we referred in Section 2.1, something that you will go on to consider in Chapter 4. It is dangerously easy for celebrities themselves, whether they are political leaders or entertainers, to believe their personal greatness is directly a consequence of the love of their people – or 'audience' as they may see it in a mass media age. This may lead to narcissism and delusions of omnipotence or the development of policies that simply respond to changing popular demands, that is, those demanded by the popular media! In fact, as we have seen, the magnetism of a celebrity's personal presence is an effect of the *mediating work* of the media. We might expect celebrities themselves to lose sight of this, so engrossed are they in the constant media attention they receive, but it is even more important that we remember this too, so that we learn to be *critical* listeners, readers and students of the media. For, as this chapter has shown, celebritisation is a matter of great social, even political, importance.

5 Conclusion

Let us highlight the main points made in this chapter. We saw that the two perspectives on celebrity outlined in Section 1 share an assumption that the present is characterised by an intense and unique interest in celebrities, so much so that we refer to a celebrity culture. But, as we have seen, historical change comprises both continuities *and* changes. Taking continuities first, we can say that fame and celebrity is now, and always has been, stage-managed and fabricated by cultural mediators – whether these are a monarch's advisors or today's public relations agencies. There was never a golden age, as the cultural decline theorists would have it, when fame simply reflected the true worth of people and their glorious deeds and did not need amplification by the available media. So, one of the most important historical continuities highlighted in this chapter is that celebrity is and always has been a product of mediation. It is too easy to project onto the past through a 'God's eye' view of the present, so that the past becomes a less sophisticated version of our present time. For example, it is clear from the reactions of people in previous periods to what was going on around them that they, like some of today's commentators, felt overwhelmed by what they regarded as the saturation coverage of celebrity. In the 1880s, for example, Henry James complained of the celebrity culture of his own time as this 'age of advertisement and newspaperism, this age of interviewing' (in Salmon, 1997, p.159). We saw that in earlier periods, such as that of Louis XIV, the use of image management was regarded as crucial to the monarch's power, similar to that for political leaders today. And, to remain with the idea of continuity, we have shown that many of the textual devices of today's celebrity were established by the early part of the twentieth century. The promotion of the film star persona by the film industry, combined with the earlier interest of popular journalism in the private lives of celebrities have created an idea of celebrity persona with which we are familiar today. It could be argued that the advent of certain uses of television and other technologies simply exacerbates this opening-up of the 'back stages' that were previously unavailable for private scrutiny.

There are also changes and discontinuities (breaks with the past) in the history of celebrity too. However, as this chapter has shown, change may not always be total – affecting all parts of a culture at the same time. Celebrity does not express a cultural Zeitgeist. Rather, as we saw in the example of the invention of the film star, it is created within specific institutions and within specific historical contexts. In Section 4 we noted that a modern mass media environment differs in some significant ways from, say, the time of Louis XIV. In recent years the power to represent politics and government has shifted from political leaders to the media; and it certainly seems as if, at the present time at least, the media use celebrity and all the values with which it is associated to frame political and social affairs.

Historical change, then, is more nuanced than in the accounts of those who refer to today as a unique celebrity culture. We find that change is piecemeal rather than total, and that elements of the old are re-combined with new developments.

We have also seen that the cultural decline and populist perspectives both have important interpretations to make of the culture of celebrity today. Depending on your view, the media's celebritisation of politics, especially their emphasis on private life and 'personality', may have negatively altered the way in which political life functions. But, while each view is perceptive, neither of them provides a complete picture of how to account for today's celebrity culture. So, some aspects of contemporary celebrity may indeed manifest an increased democratisation of our culture. At the same time, the cultural decline theorists may be right that celebritisation undermines, say, the very workings of politics, as discussed in Section 4.

It may in general be true that modern celebrity is largely built upon the decline of inherited status positions and the rise of a more socially mobile society. However, the way in which writers (Gray, 2002) extrapolate from this to argue that today's instant celebrities are equally a consequence of democratisation and social levelling is more difficult to defend. They assume that the talented and noteworthy will inevitably get the publicity they deserve as long as there are opportunities for all in a competitive celebrity market. Distinctions between celebrities, it is assumed, are a reflection of their real and important personal differences. Those of a cultural decline view see things rather differently. Theodor Adorno and Max Horkheimer (1979/1944), members of the Frankfurt School of critical sociologists in the 1930s and 1940s (see Chapter 3), were the first to argue that a star's individual persona is not a triumph of individuality but rather an illusion. It is, they argued, merely the consequence of a market that creates commodities from marginal differences. Celebrities are cultural products that are manufactured in routinised ways, planned according to a tried and tested formula that results in predictable and repetitious output. Moreover, their argument continues, the individualistic view of populist theorists obscures the important structural role played by gatekeepers such as media organisations that determine who shall become a celebrity (see Chapter 3). So, even if we acknowledge that today there are more possibilities for ordinary people to become publicly known, it does not follow that today's celebrity culture manifests increased democratisation and equal opportunities of access.

We have discussed what the concept of celebrity entails, how celebrities become permeated with social values, and how a number of commentators view celebrity culture as significant and new. But, as the next chapter argues, we need to look more closely at how celebrities actually come to our attention – that is, are brought to us as their audiences – by means of textual devices that make up the representations of them. Remeber, the vast majority of people do not encounter celebrities directly, but only indirectly through the personae created for them by a host of media producers. You have already begun to make this kind of textual analysis, but it is the special remit of Chapter 2 to show how and why texts have their own orderly structure and meaningful effects.

Further reading

Boorstin, D. (1961) *The Image: A Guide to Pseudo-Events in America*, Harmondsworth, Penguin.

Braudy, L. (1997) *Frenzy of Renown,* New York, Vintage Books.

Celdran, D. (2001) 'The cult of celebrity', *Media: The Investigative Reporting Magazine*, Philippine Centre for Investigative Journalism, January–March, vol.vii, no.1. (Accessed at http://www.pcij.org/imag/Media/celebrity.html on 19 August 2004.)

Corner, J. and Pels, D. (eds) (2003) *Media and the Restyling of Politics*, London, Sage.

Dyer, R. (1979) *Stars*, London, BFI publishing. (Reprinted in 2001.)

Gamson, J. (1992) 'The assembly line of greatness', *Critical Studies in Mass Communication*, vol.9, pp.1–24.

Gray, J. (2002) 'Ulrika is a sign that we've got it all', *New Statesman*, 28 October, pp.28–30.

Meyrowitz, J. (1985) *No Sense of Place*, Oxford, Oxford University Press.

Pels, D. (2003) 'Aesthetic representation and political style' in Corner and Pels (eds) (2003).

Schickel, R. (1985) *Common Fame: The Culture of Celebrity,* New York, Fromm International.

Turner, G., Bonner, F. and Marshall, P.D. (2000) *Fame Games: The Production of Celebrity in Australia*, Cambridge, Cambridge University Press.

Turner, G. (2004) *Understanding Celebrity*, London, Sage.

References

Adorno, T. and Horkheimer, M. (1979/1944) 'The culture industry: enlightenment as mass deception' in *Dialectic of Enlightenment,* London, Verso.

Alberoni, F. (1972) 'The powerless elite' in McQuail, D. (ed.) *Sociology of Mass Communications,* Harmondsworth, Penguin.

Balio, T. (1985) *The American Film Industry*, Madison, WI, University of Wisconsin Press.

Blumler, J.G. and Gurevitch, M. (2000) 'Rethinking the study of political communication' in Curran, J. and Gurevitch, M. (eds) *Mass Media and Society* (3rd edn) London, Edward Arnold.

Boorstin, D. (1961) *The Image: A Guide to Pseudo-Events in America*, Harmondsworth, Penguin.

Braudy, L. (1997) *Frenzy of Renown*, New York, Vintage Books.

Briggs, A. and Burke, P. (2002) *A Social History of the Media: From Gutenberg to the Internet*, Cambridge, Polity Press.

Burke, P. (1992) *The Fabrication of Louis XIV*, New Haven, CT, Yale University Press.

Celdran, D. (2001) 'The cult of celebrity', *Media: The Investigative Reporting Magazine*, Philippine Centre for Investigative Journalism, January–March, vol.vii, no.1, http://www.pcij.org/imag/Media/celebrity.html (accessed 19 August 2004).

Corner, J. and Pels, D. (eds) (2003) *Media and the Restyling of Politics*, London, Sage.

Cowen, T. (2000) *What Price Fame?*, Cambridge, MA, Harvard University Press.

Cunningham, J. (2002) 'Fame and fortune', *The Guardian (G2)*, 4 December, p.5.

deCordova, R. (1990) *Picture Personalities: The Emergence of the Star System in America*, Champaign, IL, University of Illinois Press.

deCordova, R. (1991) 'The emergence of the star system in America' in Gledhill, C. (ed.) *Stardom: Industry of Desire*, London, Routledge.

Dyer, R. (1979) *Stars*, London, BFI Publishing (reprinted in 2001).

Evans, J. (2003) Interview conducted with Claire Lewis, Celebrity Co-ordinator in Oxfam's Media Unit, Oxford, April.

Fiske, J. (1992) 'Popularity and the politics of information' in Dahlgren, P. and Sparks, C. (eds) *Journalism as Popular Culture*, London, Sage.

Frank, T. (2002) 'The rise of market populism', *The Nation*, 30 October, http://thenation.com (accessed 19 August 2004.)

Franklin, B. (1994*) Packaging Politics: Political Communications in Britain's Media Democracy,* London, Edward Arnold.

Franklin, B. (1998) *Tough on Soundbites, Tough on the Causes of Soundbites, New Labour and News Management*, London, The Catalyst Trust.

Freund, G. (1980) *Photography and Society*, London, Gordon Fraser.

Gamson, J. (2000) 'The web of celebrity', *The American Prospect*, vol.11, no.20, 11 September, http://www.prospect.org (accessed 19 August 2004).

Gamson, J. (1992) 'The assembly line of greatness', *Critical Studies in Mass Communication*, vol.9, pp.1–24.

Garratt, S. (2002) 'Idols made in our own image', *The Observer*, 3 February, p.16.

Gitlin, T. (1998) 'The culture of celebrity', *Dissent*, Summer, pp.81–3.

Gitlin, T. (2001) *Media Unlimited: How the Torrent of Images and Sounds Overwhelms our Lives*, New York, Metropolitan Books.

Gledhill, C. (1991) 'Signs of melodrama' in Gledhill, C. (ed.) *Stardom: Industry of Desire*, London, Routledge.

Gledhill, C. (1991) (ed.) *Stardom: Industry of Desire*, London, Routledge.

Gray, J. (2002) 'Ulrika is a sign that we've got it all', *New Statesman*, 28 October, pp.28–30.

Hart, R.P. (1994) *Seducing America: How Television Charms the Modern Voter*, Oxford, Oxford University Press.

Hartley, J. (1996) *Popular Reality: Journalism, Modernity, Popular Culture*, London, Edward Arnold.

Horton, D. and Wohl R.R. (1993) 'Mass communication and para-social interaction', in Corner, J. and Hawthorne, J. (eds) *Communication Studies: An Introductory Reader*, London, Edward Arnold. (First published in 1956 in *Psychiatry*, vol.19, pp.215–29.)

Lash, S. (1990) *Sociology of Postmodernism*, London, Routledge.

Liddiment, D. (2003) 'Reality TV's ultimate trick', *The Guardian (G2)*, 23 April, p.3.

Lumby, C. (1999) *Gotcha!: Life in a Tabloid World*, Sydney, Allen and Unwin.

McCann, G. (1996) *Cary Grant: A Class Apart*, New York, Columbia University Press.

MacManus, R. (2004) *Culture of Celebrity and Weblogs*, http://www.readwriteweb.com/2003/10/26.html (accessed 19 August 2004).

Marshall, P.D. (1997) *Celebrity and Power: Fame in Contemporary Society*, South Minneapolis, MN, University of Minnesota Press.

Meyrowitz, J. (1985) *No Sense of Place*, Oxford, Oxford University Press.

Milmo, C. (2003) 'Court drama: Hollywood stars take the stand and defend their lifestyle as they seek damages over a "disgusting" invasion of their privacy', *The Independent*, 11 February, p.3.

Pels, D. (2003) 'Aesthetic representation and political style' in Corner, J. and Pels, D. (eds) *Media and the Restyling of Politics*, London, Sage.

Ponce de Leon, C.L. (2002) *Self-Exposure: Human Interest Journalism and the Emergence of Celebrity in America 1890–1940*, Carolina, NC, University of North Carolina Press.

Postman, N. (1985) *Amusing Ourselves to Death*, London, Methuen.

Salmon, R. (1997) 'Signs of intimacy: the literary celebrity in the age of interviewing', *Victorian Literature and Culture*, vol.25, no.1, pp.159–77.

Scammell, M. (2003) 'Citizen consumers: towards a new marketing of politics?' in Corner, J. and Pels, D. (eds) *Media and the Restyling of Politics*, London, Sage.

Schickel, R. (1985) *Common Fame: The Culture of Celebrity*, New York, Fromm International.

Schilling, K. (2003) 'Private lessons', *The Guardian*, 14 April, http://media.guardian.co.uk (accessed 19 August 2004).

Schudson, M. (1978) *Discovering the News: A Social History of American Newspapers*, New York, Basic Books.

Sennett, R. (1977) *The Fall of Public Man*, London, Faber and Faber.

Smith, A. (2002) 'All in a good cause?', *The Observer*, 27 January, http://observer.guardian.co.uk (accessed 19 August 2004).

South, G. (2000) 'Celebrity power: why the UK's obsession with fame is becoming unhealthy', *The Business, Financial Times Weekend Magazine*, 30 September, pp.20–3.

Street, J. (2001) *Mass Media, Politics and Democracy*, Basingstoke, Palgrave.

Sturken, M. (2001) 'When "ordinary" people become famous', *Celebrity Culture and Politics*, http://learcenter.org/pdf/sturken.pdf (accessed 19 August 2004).

Thompson, J.B. (1995) *The Media and Modernity*, Cambridge, Polity Press.

Turner, G., Bonner, F. and Marshall, P.D. (2000) *Fame Games: The Production of Celebrity in Australia*, Cambridge, Cambridge University Press.

Walker, A. (1970) *Stardom: The Hollywood Phenomenon*, London, Michael Joseph.

Wells, M. and Twist, R. (2002) 'David and Victoria who?', *The Guardian* (G2), 20 May, p.8–9.

Whillock, R.K. (1999) 'Giant sucking sounds: politics as illusion' in Slayden, D. and Whillock, R.K. (eds) *Soundbite Culture: The Death of Discourse in a Wired World*, London, Sage.

The celebrity in the text

Chapter 2

Frances Bonner

Contents

1   Introduction

This chapter is concerned with the very things that we, as ordinary people, talk about as a consequence of listening to radio, watching television or reading newspapers and magazines: the programmes and articles that constitute media output. Until now we have considered an overview of the centrality of mediation to celebrity. We do not (except on rare occasions) experience celebrities face-to-face for, as Chapter 1 established, their celebrity is conditional on having their image disseminated far and wide. Here we move in closer in order to examine the everyday *evidence* of celebrity activity – what academic media analysts call 'texts'. The French literary theorist Roland Barthes (1915–1980) chose the term 'texts' to reject the idea that the author's intentions are central to our understanding of a work (the old literary studies approach) and to emphasise that the reader is also important in the meaning-making process (1977, p.148). The social situation within which the reader is making the meaning is also significant. Texts are socially constructed assemblages of items such as spoken or written words, or pictures. Within media and cultural studies, the term 'text' is now the standard way to refer to an item (such as a newspaper or magazine article, photograph or television programme), and to examine its cultural meanings. As you will see in the next two chapters, producers make products that consumers take pleasure from. But a thoroughgoing understanding of the operation of the media requires us to consider not just production and reception, but the texts that *connect* them. Texts are the (usually) material form connecting these two activities, and as such deserve and repay *separate* consideration. The next section of this chapter looks at the ways in which those who study the media analyse texts. Section 3 considers how texts can be grouped together by 'type' and categorised. Section 4 presents a sustained reading of the cultural meanings of an extended celebrity text and Section 5 looks at claims relating to the increased presence of celebrities in the news.

2   Representation and the text

2.1   The semiotic approach to textual meaning

We can talk of the process of meaning-making as one where producers *encode* information into texts and consumers *decode* meanings from them (Hall, 1980). This idea of encoding and decoding implies that the process is one-way – producers create texts that are then read by consumers – but movement can occur the other way as well: texts can be created as a response to consumers' expression of their enjoyment of existing ones and desire for similar texts (which is how producers interpret box-office figures, television ratings or top-ten lists). Features of existing texts, such as their classification into genres (science fiction, or heist movie, for example) or star image, can feed back into production, leading to certain characteristics being emphasised above others. For example, after the unexpected success of Sandra Bullock in *Speed* (1994), the film *While You Were Sleeping* (1995) was tailored as a 'star vehicle' to capitalise on her popularity and show her ability to play another 'kooky' character, but this time in the different genre of a romantic comedy.

It is important in analysing the media and in analysing celebrity not to concentrate only on the highest profile, most 'important' instances. We can learn much more about the regular operation of the media and of celebrity by looking at more ordinary, even trivial, cases. To understand this, think about Elvis Presley: we may all have some knowledge of Elvis, but we would learn little about everyday media uses of celebrity by concentrating on such an exceptional case.

Activity 2.1

Think of how you receive knowledge about and pleasure from celebrities. Is it primarily live or recorded, from performances (sporting, acting, singing) or from interviews or stories about their lives? ■ ■ ■

Although you may see celebrities physically present at a concert, a play, a sporting event or a political rally, these will almost certainly comprise the least of your encounters. For the most part your encounters are likely to be mediated electronically or through print, and these are the ones we will concentrate on here. As consumers we deal with mediated texts for much of each day; we know how to take information and entertainment from them and how to ignore them. But what do we do differently to analyse them in a more objective way?

One approach is to look at the process by which meaning is made from texts. Many tools are available (see **Gillespie and Toynbee, 2006**). Semiotics (the science of signs) was the system Barthes used to interpret or 'read' texts. This is a highly developed analytic system and we will draw on only a few of its concepts here to aid our analysis. Textual analysis is the main methodology used in this chapter; it includes semiotics and content analysis, although we shall be concentrating largely on the former. In conducting textual analysis in media studies we slow down our 'automatic' reading of a text in order to identify how it is that we make meaning from it, and also how it is that the meaning we make is likely to be similar to that made by other people from a similar culture; we may also look for major potential variants. Textual analysts do not concern themselves with idiosyncratic readings of texts, but look for common or potentially shared meanings. They do not argue that there is a single meaning for each text, but they do look for what the British cultural theorist Stuart Hall (1980, p.134) calls the 'preferred' or 'dominant' meaning, by which is meant the one encouraged by the text, the context and the medium in which it is found.

For example, look at the newspaper photograph of the Australian cricket team celebrating a Test series win in the West Indies in 2003 (see Figure 2.1). The preferred reading of this photograph would probably be that the team is relaxing, having fun after working hard for victory. Since it comes from a newspaper called *The Australian,* we can also assume that the preferred reading is that the victory was deserved and very much something to be celebrated. However, had the newspaper been West Indian, the preferred meaning may have been different. This is a first indication that textual meaning is *contextual*, not once and for all. The photograph also comes from the back page of the paper which means that it is categorised as a sporting photograph, even though no actual cricket is shown. At this point we should *slow down* our reading to recognise that we are not dealing with a universal situation, but a *convention*. It is the practice of newspapers in the English-speaking, or even the Western, world to put sports news at the back of the newspaper and to regard the back of the newspaper as that which opens on the left, yet this is the front of Japanese and Chinese newspapers. While there is some causal basis for which way a newspaper opens, located in whether the writing system employed runs from left to right or right to left, there is no such causal explanation for the placement of sports news at the back of the paper (it could easily appear in the middle), yet it has become fully naturalised to the extent that those who favour sports over other kinds of news automatically open their (English language) papers from the back.

It is also a convention that people in newspaper photographs are named, or at least those who are the subject of the photograph are, yet only one person, Steve Waugh, is named here (note that the 'text' comprises the photograph and the caption). As the captain he is arguably the most celebrated. He is placed both in the foreground and centrally (the person on the left of the two holding the trophy – the other is the then vice-captain, Ricky Ponting); this placement has encoded him as one of the two most important people in the group and the naming ensures that he gets pre-eminence. Placement is an important element of the photographic *code*, especially for (semi-) formal shots (think of the main photograph of a wedding party and what it tells us about the relationships of those depicted). Codes are more systematised than conventions – significantly so in the case of the Highway Code, which like many codes is a system of rules.

Chesty bonding: The Australian team surround Steve Waugh with the Frank Worrell Trophy in the sea at Antigua

Figure 2.1 *Australian cricket team in the sea at Antigua in 2003*

The next element of the preferred meaning of this text to consider is that it suggests through its use of this photographic code that Waugh is pre-eminently the person responsible for the team winning the Test series. Winning is shown here *metaphorically* by the trophy that Waugh holds. The trophy stands in for the process of winning, in the same way in which a rose stands in metaphorically for an expression of love. Because trophies commonly represent success, they are frequent components of the image of celebrities. The Oscars are no doubt the most famous, but award ceremonies exist for most fields from which celebrities are drawn, and photographs and television coverage of award-winners provide some of the most common images of celebrity.

Activity 2.2

Think of an image of a celebrity winning an award. How is s/he photographed, dressed and accompanied? ■ ■ ■

Perhaps the most likely image you thought of was a full-length or mid-shot of the celebrity dressed formally, smiling and holding a trophy, accompanied by some member of the opposite sex, either their partner for the evening, the person presenting the award or a fellow recipient. The ease with which you should have been able to call up such an image speaks about how pervasive it is, and how much it underwrites the way celebrities are shown as winners. The frequency with which the image places a man and a woman together indicates how strong still, despite the existence of a (very) few openly gay or lesbian celebrities, is the linkage of celebrity and heterosexuality. Because celebrities are presented to us as figures of desire (both desirable and desiring) their sexuality is an important part of the stories we are told about them. This, too, is part of the idea of the pervasive image to which we will return later.

Another set of terms drawn from semiotics that we can use to analyse texts is *denotation* and *connotation*. Although it is a simplification (see discussion in **Gillespie and Toynbee, 2006**), we can consider these as referring to the more neutral and the more culturally specific meanings in texts respectively. If the image you thought of included a red carpet, then that denotes a floor covering, but it connotes importance – we 'roll out the red carpet' only for valued guests. In the photograph of the cricketers in Figure 2.1, the tropical setting denotes Antigua, the site of the final test match, but, especially to those living far from the West Indies, it connotes a luxurious holiday. The caption about 'chesty bonding' has a culturally specific connotation for those who know the Australian advertising icon, Chesty Bond, who advertises a brand of underwear for men, also called Chesty Bond.

If the celebrity and award you thought of was from sport, you may have imagined the winning of a competition and the attire would have been different. Sporting success normally requires that the evening wear in an 'award' text be replaced by appropriate strip. This should make us focus particularly on the minimal gestures to uniform on the cricketers' part in Figure. 2.1. Part of the way in which we make meaning from texts such as this photograph comes from *contrasting* them with conventional (celebrity) photographs, and there are two main contrasts operating here. Celebrities do not commonly appear in large group photographs; far more often they appear individually or, as suggested above, as part of a couple. Cricketers, though, are members of a team before they are individuals, so while this is a contrast, it does not make a large contribution to the meaning of this text. The more significant contrast with what we expect lies in the tropical beach setting, which in turn produces, or justifies, the bare-chested shot. The caps alone represent the uniform. We call this process *metonymy*, where a part stands for the absent whole. This particular metonym is a very powerful one: it has not just been chosen for the photograph (as long as we are part of this sporting culture, we understand from everyday experience that a cap represents, or stands in for, the uniform), it exists in sporting language.

We speak of people being chosen for the national cricket team as being 'capped' for England (or Australia or the West Indies).

When we talk of an image, we should not think of it as just referring to pictures, although the physical appearance of celebrities is central to their mediated presence. Images include what we learn through the written and spoken words that accompany the visuals. In addition to the preferred (or dominant) reading, Hall (1980, p.134) also talks of oppositional and negotiated readings. These are possible because of what semiotics refers to as *polysemy* – the potential multiplicity of meanings we can take from a text. A negotiated reading is one in which the reader only partly shares the text's connotative meaning and sometimes modifies it to reflect their own position and experiences. A reading of this kind might see the Australian cricket team as an example of 'beefcake'. An oppositional reading, in which the reader's social situation places them in a directly oppositional relation to the preferred or dominant reading because they do not share it, might in this case be that the cricketers are overpaid and overfed white intruders. But we must also take into account any surrounding text or captions that provide an additional source of meaning for the image. Captions usually serve to reduce the polysemy of visuals and to reinforce – or help to create – the preferred meaning. Textual analysts refer to captions having potentially two functions in this regard. Captions may *anchor* meaning, which indicates that they 'tie down' a meaning that is already obviously available from the image and, therefore, make it more difficult for alternative meanings to emerge (Barthes, 1977). Captions may also *relay* a meaning, supplying the image with a *new* meaning that the image by itself was unlikely to have implied. The caption, with its reference to 'Chesty bonding' acts as a relay in this way. Overall, the preferred meaning of the Australian cricket team photograph, when we combine the meaning of the image and the caption, is that success in a test series requires celebration, which also involves a celebration of masculine bonding.

Dominant, oppositional and negotiated – the terms that Hall attaches to particular types of readings – refer to ideological positions. I am not using the term 'ideology' to refer to a partisan political position, but to systems of thought and belief that provide quite deeply embedded frameworks for understanding the world (Hall, 1985, p.99). John B. Thompson (1990, p.56) is emphatic in asserting that these frameworks exist in relationship to power, that they serve to support relations of domination and we can see this in the terms that Hall gives the types of readings. The dominant reading accepts the world as it is – here, that these cricketers deserve to celebrate. The oppositional reading I have suggested (and it is only one possible reading out of many) is based on a framework that sees 'race' as highly significant. The rather frivolous negotiated reading suggested disregards the importance of a national team in favour of a more sexualised world-view.

Examine the photograph of Nicole Kidman in Figure 2.2. This is taken from her appearance at Cannes in May 2003 to promote *Dogville* (France, dir. von Trier, 2003), her then new film directed by Lars von Trier. What are the important elements of this celebrity photograph? ■ ■ ■

Perhaps, as well as noting her pose, hair, attire, figure and necklace, you registered the photographers in the background. It is more common for such photographs of celebrities to have only the star in focus and blur the background; in fact this may be regarded as another element of the photographic code. Here, the photographers themselves indicate the importance of the event and the magnitude of the star, there are so many of them jostling to get the best shot. This photograph shows an example of Boorstin's pseudo-event (1961, p.49), mentioned in the Book Introduction. The celebrity is walking along a cat-walk designed to allow her to be photographed promoting her latest work. It is a *photo opportunity* pure and simple, for if there were no photographers there would be no point, as nothing else is happening. The press conferences that followed Kidman's appearance at Cannes were pseudo-events too.

Figure 2.2 *Nicole Kidman at Cannes in May 2003*

2.2 The representation of 'celebrity'

We have already seen the way in which texts gain meaning from other texts by the operation of contrast, but multiple texts are useful to the textual analyst in another way. Looking at a large number of texts dealing with the same subject – celebrity – enables us to detect common themes and narratives (stories), to the extent that with enough repetition we become able to talk about the *representation* of that subject. Working through a large number of texts about celebrities, we become aware of common themes. The stress is overwhelmingly on relationships, consumption and leisure, and work is quite minor. This is part of the establishment of a form of para-social intimacy (Horton and Wohl, 1993) with the celebrity as discussed in Chapter 1. We learn about the kinds of things we would otherwise know only about people who really were our friends. Celebrity is depicted most consistently (that is, it is a pervasive image) as a matter of enhanced opportunities for sex, romance and conspicuous display. This indicates little change from the 1920s and 1930s, the time generally seen as that in which celebrity, then called stardom, was most thoroughly developed. Drawing on popular US film magazines, Richard deCordova (1990, p.108) argues that stars were important vehicles for promoting the new consumer ideals at this time: 'In conspicuously displaying ... success through material possessions, the star vividly demonstrated the idea that satisfaction was not to be found in work but in one's activities away from work – in consumption and leisure.' As far as sex, romance and relationships are concerned, he traces a change from the 1910s to the 1920s in a shift from the earlier emphasis on marriages and happy families to a greater focus on scandals, especially sexual ones. Celebrities were and are used in media texts to promote a set of social values that see consumption, relationships and leisure as more meaningful and satisfying than work or education.

If we extend the period back to the previous century though, we do find that, like most representations, celebrity can change over time. We no longer think of celebrities as more worthy than ordinary people and, as Chapter 1 has pointed out, long-term processes such as democratisation have made a major contribution to this. David Marshall also focuses on the rise of movie stars in the 1910s but sees it as a clear sign of the decline of the nineteenth-century notion that linked public prominence to heroes and 'great men' (1997, pp.7–9). Now that we know so much about the manufacture of individual celebrities, it is hard to sustain a belief that celebrities are prominent because their talent just 'naturally' made them outstanding. The exception here is with sports stars, where the sports industry is structured to ensure that there are bases for saying that a particular performer is 'best' and for ranking the others accordingly (Giles, 2000, p.107). Sport provides more exceptions – the frequent coverage of training (at least for those few sports that are regarded as major ones) as well as the frequency of competitions, means that we do hear about the (non-celebrity) work involved and its significance. The stress on relationships and consumption remains, though.

The majority of celebrity coverage is the result of highly *managed* media occasions – red carpet appearances such as Kidman's at Cannes discussed above, interviews and photo-shoots such as those in *Hello!* magazine discussed in Chapter 1 and the staged appearance on selected chat-shows. Very famous celebrities may wield considerable control over their publicity, even demanding final approval of both stories and photographs under pain of blacklisting the non-compliant outlet. However, there is a body of texts that is not authorised by the celebrity and her or his management. These include gossip items, unflattering photographs from public events and photographs taken by paparazzi. Alan Sekula (1984, p.29) has commented on 'the higher truth of the stolen image', noting how the unauthorised photograph 'is thought to manifest more of the "inner being" of the subject than is the calculated gestalt of immobilized gesture, expression and stance'. To maintain this aspect, editors may retain elements of unauthorised photographs such as bad framing, or may choose shots that are not well focused, to emphasise their 'stolen' nature. They can be regarded as debunking the 'mystique' of the celebrity, and though there are few signs that such coverage acts to disqualify a person from celebrity status, it may inflect their image somewhat. Police reports and pictures about the illegal activities of Hugh Grant or Robert Downey Jr have not been detrimental to their popularity or earning power, indeed they may even have benefited Grant.

Activity 2.4

Look at the photograph of Goldie Hawn and its accompanying caption (see Figure 2.3). This is from a regular section in the gossip magazine *Heat* entitled 'Scandal', where unflattering photographs, not all of them paparazzi ones, are printed with snide comments and admonitions. The magazine obviously thinks Hawn has done something wrong. What set of social values do you think Hawn is said to have transgressed? ■ ■ ■

Hawn's celebrity image has for many years focused on how young she looks for her age, and here she is being taken to task not only for a lack of taste (celebrities are supposed to be constantly fashionable and are regularly castigated for lapses), but because of age-inappropriate dressing. Most of the instances where magazines turn moralistic about appearance in this way concern female celebrities. It is an indication of the continuing

Why on earth is Goldie Hawn wearing a maternity frock? After all, her daughter's pregnant, not her. We know she's halfway to finding the secret of eternal youth, but even she has to admit that the odds of her giving birth again are rather slim. Billowing nightie aside, those Eurotrash jeans are appalling, the shoes are super-tacky and ditto the necklace. In fact, the only tasteful thing about the outfit is the Marni jacket she's trailing behind her. A warped sense of priorities if ever we saw one.

Figure 2.3 *This photograph of Goldie Hawn and accompanying caption appeared in* Heat *magazine in 2003*

force of an ideology that holds women as *embodied*, that is determined by their physical being, far more than is the case for men.

Looking across a number of texts enables us to build a picture of how an abstract phenomenon such as celebrity is generally represented. We can then feed this back into our analysis of individual texts (as we did with Hawn) to observe how they may act to differentiate and individualise particular celebrities one from another, and provide each with a persona – a major part of the process of 'celebritisation' as noted in Chapter 1. A single long-lasting marriage may be the focus of one celebrity's image simply because of the contrast to the pervasive image of celebrities having many relationships.

As a celebrity 'emerges' – a result of considerable work on their own part and that of the producers who work with them (see Chapter 3) – and as the public starts to recognise them, their image does not develop from a blank slate. On the one hand there is the person with certain skills and physical characteristics, and on the other a culture already operating various systems of representation, such as those relating to gender, 'race', sexuality and of course celebrity itself. Producers developing the celebrity of a particular person are circumscribed in their activities by pre-existing texts, representations and ideologies. They need both to *individualise* their client and to fit her/him into existing beliefs. Once a celebrity has been established with certain qualities, these help determine subsequent deployment (see the Oxfam example in Chapter 1, Section 4, and the further discussion in the Conclusion).

Activity 2.5

Consider the UK television celebrity Carol Vorderman. Where does she appear? What qualities are most associated with her? (If she is unfamiliar to you, think of another highly visible television presenter.) ■ ■ ■

Do not worry if you have not heard of Carol Vorderman. By choosing another, highly visible presenter, you should still be able to extract the point of this example, which is that celebrities have to be individualised, but also gain meaning from the way they fit into or alter existing beliefs. To my mind, the prime qualities of Carol Vorderman are her femininity and her mathematical skill, and so, although she is used across a range of genres and texts (as well as her core presence as co-presenter of the Channel 4 quiz show *Countdown* there have been advertisements for mathematics teaching systems and various science and technology programmes), producers deciding whether to use her in a particular product have to take account of these qualities. Even in a programme that seemed to represent her break away from 'science and maths', *Carol Vorderman's Better Homes* (ITV1), she was associated with a makeover programme in which improvement was measured numerically (in this context as an increase in house valuation). Preceding this individualisation of Vorderman, there is a gendered representation, a stereotype, that says women are not good at mathematics. This does not prohibit Vorderman from appearing publicly as a woman performing rapid mental arithmetic: instead it makes it possible to highlight this aspect of her presentation as different and special – and thus central to her persona.

She is, then, much more distinctive and marketable than a man doing the same thing. She can even be deployed to counter the stereotype and try to break it down by demonstrating that it is inaccurate and by encouraging other women, especially those in younger age groups, to do well at mathematics. (Similarly, Jamie Oliver first came to prominence in *The Naked Chef*, marked by a cheeky persona and a can-do approach to cooking. His subsequent modulation into the more socially aware person, training the unemployed for restaurant work, used both of these qualities to bring him closer to the apprentices and to contest the stereotypical image of the do-gooder.)

The two examples indicate ways in which celebrities can draw on or counteract social stereotypes – particular kinds of representations that usually serve to characterise members of particular social groups by a limited number of traits. Stereotypes are usually perceived as negative constructs; they serve to speed communication and reinforce shared values. Stereotypes are ideological concepts, for they are deeply rooted in social beliefs. T.E. Perkins (1979, p.141) notes that the resilience and power of a stereotype 'result from a combination of three factors: its simplicity; its immediate recognisability (which makes its communicative role very important); and its implicit reference to an assumed consensus about some attribute or complex social relationships.' A person described in the British media as a 'fundamentalist' (of whatever kind) is unlikely to be presented as praiseworthy or as similar to the people likely to be the majority of that outlet's audience. This simple process of naming will have conveyed, with considerable efficiency, the point about the person's supposed extremism and resistance to rational argument.

Reading 2.1 Activity

Now read the following extract from Richard Dyer, 'Stars as types' (Reading 2.1). As you read, consider the following questions and make notes:

■ What does Dyer suggest we bear in mind when using the concept of social types?

■ How much of the description of the pin-up he provides from Hess remains applicable today?

■ Try to identify two social types that are exemplified by current celebrities.

Reading 2.1

Richard Dyer, 'Stars as types'

Despite the extravagant lifestyle of the stars, elements such as the rags-to-riches motif and romance as an enactment of the problems of heterosexual monogamy suggest that what is important about the stars, especially in their particularity, is their typicality or representativeness. Stars, in other words, relate to the social types of a society.

The notion of social type

The notion of a type – or rather social type – has been developed by O.E. Klapp [...]

In *Heroes, Villains and Fools*, Klapp defines a social type as 'a collective norm of role behaviour formed and used by the group: an idealised concept of how people are expected to be or to act' (p.11).

It is a shared, recognisable, easily-grasped image of how people are in society (with collective approval or disapproval built into it).

On the basis of this Klapp proceeds to provide a typology of the prevalent social types in America, and he frequently provides stars' names to illustrate the different social types. Thus under 'heroes of social acceptability', he lists Will Rogers, [...] and Perry Como, and under 'snobs' he lists Grace Kelly, Elizabeth Taylor, Ingrid Bergman, [...] Katharine Hepburn, Garbo and Davis. (A star may of course be listed under several different, even contradictory categories, reflecting both the ambiguity of their image and the differences in audience attitudes – thus Monroe for instance is used as an example of 'love queen' and 'simpleton' [...] The star both fulfils/incarnates the type and, by virtue of her/his idiosyncrasies, individuates it. (Critics committed to individualism as a philosophy or tenet of common sense tend to speak of the star's individuation of a type as 'transcendence'.)

There are problems with Klapp's work. Firstly, he does not explore the sources of social types, seeing them simply as 'collective representations'. He sees social types as positive and useful, as opposed to stereotypes, which are wrong and harmful because they deal with people 'outside of one's cultural world' – yet he never examines just who is within and without the 'cultural world'. That is, he never examines the possibility that the cultural world articulated by social types may represent the hegemony of one section of society over another. Yet it is clear from his typology that if you are not white, middle class, heterosexual and male you are not going to fit 'the cultural world' too well – women only fit uneasily, whilst blacks, gays and even the working class hardly fit at all. [...] Secondly, one does rather wonder where his categories come from, how he arrived at them. There is no discussion of methodology in his writings.

Nevertheless, despite all this, one can I think *use* Klapp's typology as a description of prevalent social types, providing one conceptualises this ideologically (i.e. he is describing the type system subscribed to by the dominant groups in society) and of course allows for modifications and additions since he wrote.

Three prevalent social types as defined by Klapp are the Good Joe, the Tough Guy, and the Pin-up.

[...]

The pin-up

As already mentioned, Klapp's typology is noticeably short on women. He points out that, because 'It is still a man's world when it comes to handing out the medals' (p.97), there are particularly few women hero types, resulting in the dilemma of modern woman's 'loss of identity' (p.98). (He does not get very far in asking why this should be so – but he did observe it at a time when few other writers were doing so.) It is interesting to note that when he does propose a predominantly female type, it is one that exists primarily in media representation – the pin-up. (He could perhaps have used the term 'glamour girl'.)

Although he does include some men in his list of synonyms of the pin-up, the emphasis is on women:

> Such a model of bodily perfection need be neither a great lover nor a social lion. Photogenic perfection is enough. It may be surprising to say that a pin-up need not be unusual even in looks (many people have complained of the monotony of American cheesecake and Hollywood beauty). Fashion, cosmetology and hair styling actually increase the resemblance of pin-up types.
>
> Klapp, p.39

One might say, with heroes like that, who needs villains and fools? As a social model, the pin-up promotes surface appearance and depersonalisation, woman as sexual spectacle and sex object.

The pin-up is an important part of the way a star's image is built up, but we should not confuse this with the pin-up as a social type. All the stars we are concentrating on in this study, men as well as women, have had pin-up photographs taken and used, but of these only Monroe and Fonda were 'pin-ups'. They conformed, in their pin-up photos, to the conventions described by Thomas B. Hess in 'Pin-up and Icon':

> By the 1940s, the pin-up image was defined with canonical strictness. First of all, there was the 'pin-up girl' herself. She had to be the healthy, American, cheerleader type – button-nosed, wide-eyed, long-legged, ample hips and breasts, and above all with the open, friendly smile that discloses perfect, even, white teeth. Then there is her costume and pose. These must be inviting but not seducing; affectionate but not passionate, revealing by suggestion while concealing in fact. ... The body is evident beneath the costume, but not its details – the bulges of nipples or the *mons veneris* are scrupulously hidden. There is a dialectical pressure at work, between the voyeuristic public which wants to see more and more, and that same public which, in its social function, supports codes and laws that ban any such revelations. [...]
>
> Hess, 1972, p.227

[...]

Alternative or subversive types

Most types discussed by Klapp, and indeed most stars discussed as social types, are seen as representing dominant values in society, by affirming what those values are in the 'hero' types (including those values that are relatively appropriate to men and women) and by denouncing other values in the villain and fool types. Klapp argues, however, that there may also be other types that express discontent with or rejection of dominant values. These types will also be grounded in a normative world-view [that is, from within an implicit value system], but as an alternative to the dominant one.

References

Hess, T.B. (1972) 'Pin-up and Icon' in Hess, T.B. and Nochlin, L. (eds) *Woman as Sex Object*, New York, Newsweek.

Klapp, O.E. (1962) *Heroes, Villains and Fools*, Prentice-Hall, Englewood Cliff, NJ.

Reading source

Dyer, 1998, pp.47–52 ■ ■ ■

'Stars as types' was first published in 1979 (and the Klapp work Dyer discusses comes from 1962) and deals only with film stars, but is readily extended to other kinds of celebrity even now, as long as we take the cautious approach Dyer recommends. Dyer recognises that social types are ideological and speak primarily of dominant systems of beliefs. He suggests they can also represent alternative value systems (negotiated or oppositional), and he proposes two alternative types: the rebel (he instances James Dean while we could probably list a number of rap artists); and the independent woman. As an example of the latter he mentions Jane Fonda, but social change consequent on feminism has rendered both the example and the category far less useful. The pin-up, even if most of the details have changed, remains with us. This will be discussed further in Section 3.

We have seen, in this section, how texts can be analysed by paying close attention to their content and the implications of it, and how looking at a number of related texts enables us to discuss representations.

3 Categorising texts

Whether we are producing, analysing or consuming texts, one of the principal ways in which we make them meaningful is by considering what type of text we are dealing with. This helps to identify appropriate codes so we do not try to make meanings by calling on unsuitable frames of reference by, for example, analysing the items in a gossip magazine as if they had been subject to exhaustive checking for verifiable facts. There are many ways to categorise texts, a few of which are examined next.

3.1 By medium

We can divide texts up by the medium in which they appear. This is a broad division that is technologically based. It may seem excessively obvious, but it can be quite revealing. For example, different media have different periodicities (frequency of appearances) – most magazines appear weekly or monthly, while newspapers are weekly or daily. Episodes of television programmes are most commonly also weekly or daily, but films appear on a different basis altogether, since, like books or CDs they appear as single texts, not as a collection of disparate but contiguous texts held together by the technology of the medium itself. Some people talk about these latter as 'everyday media' since we encounter them more regularly (see Bonner, 2003). One consequence of varying periodicities for consideration of celebrity is that promotion of the single texts most commonly occurs in the continuous media. Films and books are regularly discussed on radio, in the newspapers and on television in a way that is very different from the occasional use of television or radio in films. One result is to make the everyday media appear to be in the service of the more sporadic ones. We must be careful though to note how a single text may appear in different formats, which may involve different media. A successful television programme, such as a nature documentary (everyday media) presented by David Attenborough, will also be released on video and DVD, accompanied by a book of the series and perhaps a separate recording of the music from it (that is, as single texts). The celebrity figure of Attenborough is, however, an integral part of the promotion of each format.

The terms 'film star', 'television presenter' and 'recording artist' name different types of celebrities by virtue of the medium in which their appearance is deemed central, although texts about them can be found far more widely. In the early work of media studies theorists, there was a distinction between film 'stars' and television 'personalities' based on the distance between stars and their audiences compared to the familiarity and intimacy viewers felt with television personalities (Langer, 1981). This distinction is now outdated (though see the discussion in Chapter 3) because the widespread use of the term 'celebrity' to name both categories indicates how individual celebrities are rarely restricted to a single medium now. Traces of it remain, however, and are evident in a story George Clooney told in an interview (Vincent, 2003) about being familiarly greeted by fans who felt his regular presence in their homes (in *ER*) meant he was one of them compared to Mel Gibson who was respectfully left alone.

3.2 By genre

A second categorisation which operates on the 'type' of text involved is *genre*. Most writing on genre looks either at literature or film, yet it can equally be used for other media. In the following reading, Steve Neale places much importance on what he calls 'intertextual relay', where links *between* a number of texts are made explicit, for example by the marketing of cultural products. In this way the expectations of viewers and readers are channelled; they can therefore come to recognise in advance what type of text they will encounter.

Reading 2.2 Activity

Now read the following extract from Steven Neale, 'Questions of genre' (Reading 2.2). As you read consider the following questions and pay particular attention to what Neale says about the 'intertextual relay', since this will be discussed below.

- Genres are not just texts, what else are they and why is this important?
- Why are genres useful?
- What does 'verisimilitude' mean? What are the two main types of it?
- What does the term 'narrative image' refer to?

Reading 2.2

Steve Neale, 'Questions of genre'

Expectations and verisimilitude

There are several general, conceptual points to make at the outset. The first is that genres are not simply bodies of work or groups of films, however classified, labelled and defined. Genres do not consist only of films: they consist also, and equally, of specific systems of expectation and hypothesis which spectators bring with them to the cinema, and which interact with films themselves during the course of the viewing process. These systems provide spectators with means of recognition and understanding. They help render films, and the elements within them, intelligible and therefore explicable. They offer a way of working out the significance of what is happening on the screen: a way of working out why particular events and actions are taking place, why the characters are dressed the way they are, why they look, speak and behave the way they do, and so on. Thus, if, for instance, a character in a film for no reason (or no otherwise explicable reason) bursts into song, the spectator is likely to hypothesise that the film is a musical, a particular kind of film in which otherwise unmotivated singing is likely to occur. These systems also offer grounds for further anticipation. If a film is a musical, more singing is likely to occur, and the plot is likely to follow some directions rather than others.

Inasmuch as this is the case, these systems of expectation and hypothesis involve a knowledge of – indeed they partly embody – various regimes of verisimilitude, various systems of plausibility, motivation, justification and belief. Verisimilitude means 'probable' or 'likely'.[1] It entails notions of propriety, of what is appropriate and *therefore* probable (or probable and therefore appropriate).

Regimes of verisimilitude vary from genre to genre. (Bursting into song is appropriate, therefore probable – therefore intelligible, therefore believable – in a musical. Less so in a thriller or a war film.) As such these regimes entail rules, norms and laws. (Singing in a musical is not just a probability, it is a necessity. It is not just likely to occur, it is bound to.) As Tzvetan Todorov, in particular, has insisted, there are two types of verisimilitude applicable to representations: generic verisimilitude on the one hand, and, on the other, a broader social or cultural verisimilitude. Neither equates in any direct sense to 'reality' or 'truth'.

[...] it is often the generically verisimilitudinous ingredients of a film, the ingredients, that is, which are often least compatible with regimes of cultural verisimilitude – singing and dancing in the musical, the appearance of the monster in the horror film – that constitute its pleasure, and that thus attract audiences to the film in the first place. They too, therefore, tend to be 'public', known, at least to some extent, in advance.

[...]

Genre and institutional discourse

As John Ellis has pointed out, central to the practices of the film industry is the construction of a 'narrative image' for each individual film:

> An idea of the film is widely circulated and promoted, an idea which can be called the 'narrative image' of the film, the cinema's anticipatory reply to the question, 'What is the film like?'
>
> Ellis, 1981, p.30

The discourse of film industry publicity and marketing play a key role in the construction of such narrative images; but important, too, are other institutionalised public discourses, especially those of the press and television, and the 'unofficial', 'word of mouth' discourses of everyday life.

Genre is, of course, an important ingredient in any film's narrative image. The indication of relevant generic characteristics is therefore one of the most important functions that advertisements, stills, reviews and posters perform. Reviews nearly always contain terms indicative of a film's generic status, while posters usually offer verbal generic (and hyperbolic) description – 'The Greatest War Picture Ever Made' – as anchorage for the generic iconography in pictorial form.

These various verbal and pictorial descriptions form what Gregory Lukow and Steven Ricci have called the cinema's 'intertextual relay' (Lukow and Ricci, 1984). This relay performs an additional, generic function: not only does it define and circulate narrative images for individual films, beginning the immediate narrative process of expectation and anticipation, it also helps to define and circulate, in combination with the films themselves, what one might call 'generic images', providing sets of labels, terms and expectations which will come to characterise the genre as a whole.

[...]

Genre as process

It may at first sight seem as though repetition and sameness are the primary hallmarks of genres: as though, therefore, genres are above all inherently static. But as Hans Robert Jauss and Ralph Cohen (and I myself) have argued (Cohen 1986, pp.205–6; Jauss, 1982, p.80; Neale, 1980, p.19), genres are, nevertheless best understood as *processes*. These processes may, for sure, be dominated by repetition, but they are also marked fundamentally by difference, variation and change.

The process-like nature of genres manifests itself as an interaction between three levels: the level of expectation, the level of the generic corpus, and the level of the 'rules' or 'norms' that govern both. Each new genre film constitutes an addition to an existing generic corpus and involves a selection from the repertoire of generic elements available at any one point in time. Some elements are included; others are excluded. Indeed some are mutually exclusive: at most points in its history, the horror film has had to characterise its monster *either* supernaturally – as in *Dracula* (1930) – *or* psychologically – as in *Psycho* (1960). In addition, each new genre film tends to extend this repertoire, either by adding a new element or by transgressing one of the old ones. Thus, for instance, *Halloween* (1979) transgressed the division between psychological and supernatural monsters, giving its monster the attributes of both. In this way the elements and conventions of a genre are always *in* play rather than being, simply *re*-played;[2] and any generic corpus is always being expanded.

Memories of the films within a corpus constitute one of the bases of generic expectation. So, too, does the stock of generic images produced by advertisements, posters and the like. As both corpus and image expand and change with the appearance of new films, new advertising campaigns, new reviews, so also what Jauss has termed the 'horizon of expectation' appropriate to each genre expands and changes as well:

> ... the relationship between the individual text and the series of texts formative of a genre presents itself as a process of the continual founding and altering of horizons. The new text evokes for the reader (or listener) the horizon of expectations and 'rules of the game' familiar to him from earlier texts, which as such can then be varied, extended, corrected, but also transformed, crossed out, or simply reproduced.
>
> Jauss, 1982, p.79

This is one reason why it is so difficult to list exhaustively the characteristic components of individual genres, or to define them in anything other than the most banal or tautological terms: a Western is a film set on the American Western frontier; a war film is a film that represents the waging of war; a detective film is a film about the investigation of criminals and crime, and so on. [...]

Exclusive definitions, lists of *exclusive* characteristics, are particularly hard to produce. At what point do Westerns become musicals like *Oklahoma!* (1955) or *Paint Your Wagon* (1969) or *Seven Brides for Seven Brothers* (1954)? At what point do singing Westerns become musicals? A what point do comedies with songs (like *A Night at the Opera* (1935)) become musical comedies? And so on.

These examples all, of course, do more than indicate the process-like nature of individual genres. They also indicate the extent to which individual genres not only form part of a generic regime, but also themselves change, develop and vary by borrowing from, and overlapping with, one another. Hybrids are by no means the rarity in Hollywood many books and articles on genre in the cinema would have us believe. This is one reason why, as Mark Vernet has pointed out, 'a guide to film screenings will often offer to the spectator rubrics like: Western, detective film, horror film, and comedy; but also: dramatic comedy, psychological drama, or even erotic detective film' [...] (Vernet, 1978).

[...] It is indeed, therefore, the case that mass-produced, popular genres have to be understood within an economic context, as conditioned by specific economic imperatives and by specific economic contradictions – in particular, of course, those that operate within specific institutions and industries. That is why it is important to stress the financial advantages to the film industry of an aesthetic regime based on regulated difference, contained variety, pre-sold expectations, and the re-use of resources in labour and materials. It is also why it is important to stress the peculiar nature of films as *aesthetic* commodities, commodities demanding at least a degree of novelty and difference from one to another and why it is necessary to explore the analogies and the distinctions between cycles and genres in the cinema, on the one hand, and models and lines in the field of non-artistic commodity production, on the other.

Notes

1 For discussions of verisimilitude and genre see Ben Brewster, 'Film', in Dan Cohn-Sherbok and Michael Irwin (eds) (1987) *Exploring Reality*, London, Allen & Unwin (esp. pp.147–9); Gerard Genette (1969) 'Vraisemblance et motivation', *Figures*, vol.3; and Tzvetan Todorov (1977) 'The typology of detective fiction' and 'An introduction to verisimilitude' in *The Poetics of Prose*, Ithaca, Cornell University Press; and Tzvetan Todorov (1981) *Introduction to Poetics*, Brighton, The Harvester Press (esp. pp.118–19).
2 I owe this phrase to an unpublished lecture on genre by Elizabeth Cowie.

References

Cohen, R. (1986) 'History and genre', *New Literary History*, vol.17, no.2, pp.205–6

Ellis, J. (1981) *Visible Fictions: Cinema: Television: Video*, London, Routledge.

Jauss, H.R. (1982) *Towards an Aesthetic of Reception*, Brighton, The Harvester Press.

Neale, S. (1980) *Genre*, London, BFI Publishing.

Lukow, G. and Ricci, S. (1984) 'The "audience" goes "public": intertextuality, genre and the responsibilities of film literacy', *On Film*, no.12, p.29.

Vernet, M. (1978) 'Genre', *Film Reader 3*, February, p.13.

Reading source
Neale, 1990, pp.45–66 ■ ■ ■

Little of Neale's very influential essay from which Reading 2.2 is extracted aims to describes the characteristics of particular genres – the reference to singing in the musical is as precise about this common way of considering genre as he gets here. At the core of his way of conceptualising the term is the idea of the implicit contract between producers and consumers about what is involved in naming a text as a member of a genre. This avoids the highly prescriptive kind of genre study that involves delineating a set of characteristics of a Western, say, in terms of iconography (guns, horses, desert), theme (the triumph of the good over the bad) and characters (the lone gunslinger) in favour of something much more fluid, which allows for the rapid modulation of genres over time. Genres are dynamic. A radical departure from what is expected may prove to be so successful that elements are incorporated into subsequent texts. Eventually, the radical becomes so conventional that it is difficult to see from the present where the original radicalness was located. The wisecracking hero of action films was uncommon before Bruce Willis embodied him in *Die Hard* (USA, dir. McTierman, 1988) (though he had been a feature of film noir), now he provides generic verisimilitude.

Earlier, in *Genre* (1980), Neale noted that genres were instances of repetition and difference, and he argued that it was not the repetition that was especially important for genre but the difference (pp.48–51). Meaning and pleasure are generated by the difference in the new genre text from the previous one encountered: if there were only repetition, the text would be boring. We go to watch a new musical or horror film to see what new wrinkles have been introduced, although we also want the elements central to the genre (singing or being frightened) to still be there. Stars can be one possible repeated aspect of particular genres at certain times. The presence of Arnold Schwarzenegger indicated an action film during the 1980s and 1990s as clearly as Bette Davis had marked a woman's melodrama during the 1940s. Some stars attempt to extend their range and aim for a greater generic diversity. Jim Carrey, who became famous in slapstick roles, appears also in other comedic genres, but usually finds his greatest hits when he returns to slapstick. This is an instance of consumers' pleasure in a type of performance influencing the continued production of particular sub-generic texts.

We can recognise the repertoire of elements and the styles common to such genres as: the interview, the review, the news item, the gossip piece, the posed photograph and the paparazzi shot; and our expectations about what will constitute each genre at particular times and in particular places is pretty clear.

Most journalistic genres modulate according to the style of the outlet in or on which they appear. A celebrity interview in a magazine like *Sneak* aimed at young women, will be stylistically very different from one in a quality Sunday paper. Sally Vincent opens an interview with George Clooney with a reflexive comment about the relationship between fans and celebrities: 'Fans are three-deep on the pavement outside Claridge's … gazing stolidly at the front entrance. If they wanted to they could saunter through its lobbies and vestibules, seek out their idol, have a good gawp. No one would stop them. But they do not want to. Thresholds are what we have the famous for' (2003, p.18). Vincent continues to use Clooney to reflect on the phenomenon of celebrity over a number of columns of predominantly small print, in a way that would be completely out of place in the pages of a girls' magazine where the longest article about the latest teenage heart-throb covers two pages with the text broken up by pictures, break-out boxes and sub-headings such as 'He's not vain!'. What we see here is the construction of texts in terms of their target audience, the audience that producers imagine (sometimes supported by survey data and focus groups) read their magazines. Indeed, in Chapter 4 we shall see that audiences do not necessarily operate in the ways producers envisage.

Genre is one of the aspects most stressed by Lukow and Ricci's (1984) concept of the 'intertextual relay' mentioned in Reading 2.2 to describe the elements that guide us into and set up each viewing experience of a film.

Activity 2.6

Look in a television and/or radio guide for an article promoting a new programme. Identify aspects of the intertextual relay, such as references to genre, known performers or other links to previous successes. ■ ■ ■

Referring to television, Andrew Tolson (1996, pp.97–100) examines the way in which the *Radio Times*, and to a lesser extent other print media outlets, guide their readers towards a new television programme, in particular by placing it generically. Tolson's example is a hospital drama that is repeatedly contrasted with the long-running show, *Casualty* (UK, BBC, 1986 to present). As well as using genre, the intertextual relay frequently encourages us to view a new programme because it features a known celebrity, by comments such as 'Charlie Dimmock, from *Ground Force*, stars here in her own show *Charlie's Water Gardens*'. The relay is a unidirectional concept aimed at providing an audience for a new cultural product; it applies equally well to musical performance and literary fiction (the Booker Prize is an important part of the intertextual relay for new books). Chat-shows are also part of the intertextual relay. In celebrity interviews, insights into the private life are tendered in return for the opportunity to promote a product or a cause at the start of the exchange. The chat-show genre strongly prioritises the private life in this exchange.

The intertextual relay properly refers to explicitly linked texts (*Casualty* is explicitly mentioned in reviews of the programme examined by Tolson). But, the links between different cultural texts that operate beyond this can be examined as instances of *intertextuality*, which refers to the process by which texts convey meaning by often implicit references to other texts or genres. *Star Trek: The Next Generation* (USA, syndicated, 1987 to present) was able to call intertextually on well-known characteristics of Shakespearean plays simply through the casting of Patrick Stewart as Captain Jean-Luc Picard and publicity about his past as a Shakespearean actor. One of the most heavily intertextual television programmes is *The Simpsons* (USA, Fox, 1989 to present) which repeatedly constructs its scripts around already existing texts such as *Citizen Kane* (USA, dir. Wells, 1941), but without in most instances explicitly naming them. The resultant episode of *The Simpsons* is completely understandable by an audience member who has no knowledge of the film, but the text is so much richer for those who are familiar with it. The same applies for viewers familiar with the celebrities whose voices and celebrity images are incorporated into the programme.

Intertextuality is a very powerful characteristic of contemporary media texts: you could envisage it as a very messy web pulling texts closer together through assumptions about their viewers' knowledge of other texts. Genre is one of the threads of such a web. It is a highly significant way in which texts convey meaning quickly and efficiently.

3.3 As core or secondary texts

The final categorisation of texts is especially useful when looking at celebrity texts. It allows us to distinguish between:

- the 'core' texts representing the work (the films, television shows, sound recordings, books, sporting performances) which provide the basis on which the individual's celebrity is founded; and

- the secondary texts of several genres (including gossip ones) which promote the core works and/or the celebrity her- or himself.

This is an adaption of a three-part division developed by John Fiske (1987, pp.84–5) which refers to primary (rather than 'core') texts and adds an extra 'tertiary' level to indicate texts constructed by the audience, which range from conversations about what we term the core texts, to the production of fan fiction: the latter is the concern of Chapter 4.

So far we have talked of secondary texts as being generated to promote core texts, but since they are produced even when there are no core texts to promote, or when the celebrity is only a socialite, we have to expand their *raison d'être* a little. Certainly they work to maintain celebrities' profiles between projects (though socialites do not have these), but this too is a production reason and I argued at the start of this chapter against seeing communication as a one-way flow. Lynn Barber (1998, p.ix), renowned celebrity interviewer, has said that she 'can make a quasi-serious case for the value of newspaper interviews as a way of celebrating the individual and discussing aspects of personal life that would otherwise be dumped into the ghetto of the women's pages. But actually the only good reason for reading celebrity interviews (or writing them) is for entertainment.' At least as much as core texts, then, secondary texts provide entertainment.

Looking at ways of categorising media texts provides us with ways of understanding how they make meanings and how they relate to one another. Some of the characteristics of particular texts derive from the medium in which they are found, while others relate to whether their function is to promote or to be the product promoted. Categorising texts by genre is a major way of handling uncertainty – enabling producers to try to meet consumers' demands and consumers to navigate through the massive number of competing texts, something that is discussed further in the next chapter. Celebrities may also be seen as 'navigational' aids, but, as we have seen, they interact with genre quite substantially.

4   The celebrity persona and the celebrity text

It has been emphasised that we can only know stars through media texts (Dyer, 1998, see also Chapter 1) and this can be extended to seeing celebrities themselves as texts, though for celebrities of any longevity we would certainly have to consider them as large, complex and modulating ones. This section will look at how we might go about reading such a text. Chapter 1 introduced the distinction between the 'real' person and a persona presented in the public arena. One pervasive feature of the 'large celebrity text' is the many ways in which it attempts to bridge this divide. The glimpses of the 'private' life in individual secondary texts from carefully managed sources ostensibly offer audiences access to the 'real' person behind the celebrity. A large celebrity text is composed of many core and secondary texts ranging across media and genres, modulating over time and across countries as aspects of the person and the persona change. To demonstrate this we will examine the long celebrity career of singer Kylie Minogue, who began as a child actor in 1980.

The core texts which underpin Kylie Minogue's celebrity include: her role as the mechanic Charlene in the TV programme *Neighbours*; her many number one pop songs including 'I should be so lucky' from her time with the Stock-Aitken-Waterman music production company in the late 1980s and 'Spinning around' of 2000 plus the various tours, videos and television appearances in which she sings them; the albums, such as *Kylie* (the biggest-selling album in the UK in 1988); her appearances at the Sydney Gay and Lesbian Mardi Gras parties following her shift to a more disco style, resulting in a significant gay following; recordings and live appearances with Nick Cave; her films (including *The Delinquents* (1989), *Streetfighter* (1994) and *Moulin Rouge* (2001)); and the 'Love Kylie' underwear line. Although she is based in England, where most of her music originates, Kylie's career began in Australia and her acting roles have been filmed there. At the end of 2002 she made news with the announcement that she had leapt from 40th to 25th on the UK list of most popular chart stars of all time.

Since many secondary texts are produced in the process of selling each of the core ones and there are significant numbers of additional ones following the celebrity through their public and private life, the quantity of secondary texts available for a celebrity of any longevity (such as Kylie Minogue) is very considerable indeed. Stories about her private life surround and exceed her varied acting and musical performances, and we can draw on some of these to consider both changes over time and how core and secondary texts interact. Brian Walsh, the principal initial publicist for *Neighbours* (Australia, Grundy, 1985 to present), outlined how in the late 1980s the (real-life) romance between Kylie and fellow *Neighbours* actor Jason Donovan was concealed for four years until following a series of hints, it could be revealed to the maximum benefit of the programme's ratings (Turner et al., 2000, pp.103–4). This was unlike her subsequent relationships, for example with INXS rock star Michael Hutchence, or with James Gooding who published an exposé of their relationship in the British tabloids in 2003. By the 1990s, speculations about celebrities' love lives were media staples, although Kylie actually receives more coverage on other issues. Most notably her battle with breast cancer in 2005.

A constant theme of the secondary texts is her diminutive size. This was capitalised on when she launched the two-seater StreetKa at the Paris Motor Show in 2002 (see Figure 2.4), where Kylie personified its urban manoeuvrability.

Fashion is another theme, since despite her height, she is persistently used in fashion shoots and on magazine covers. She has been significant in the growth of the symbiosis between fashion designers and entertainers with celebrities sitting in the front row of fashion shows and designers dressing celebrities for awards shows (see Figure 2.5). Her launch of an underwear line followed logically from this development and the 2000 shift in her image to emphasise her bottom.

Figure 2.4 Kylie Minogue advertises the StreetKa

Activity 2.7

Spend a few minutes looking at the four album covers in Figure 2.5: *Kylie*, her 1988 debut, and *Kylie Minogue* from 1994 after her break with Stock-Aitken-Waterman; then *Fever* (2001) and *Body Language* (2003). How do the images show the shifts in Kylie's career mentioned earlier? To what extent do the last two exemplify the pin-up pose outlined by Hess in Reading 2.1? ▪▪▪

Recalling the previous discussion of social type, we can plot a trajectory of Kylie's persona over the period that she has been a celebrity. She has moved from the teenage, suburban Australian ordinariness of the *Neighbours* period into the brainless, breathless Australian of her early years as a young singer in the UK, where the first album cover shows simply a head and shoulders shot with big hair. There is the arrival of sexiness through her liaison with Michael Hutchence and the transmutation into gay diva, which starts about the time of *Kylie Minogue* (1994) – a dramatic visual change with her occupying little of the frame, apparently crawling towards camera. The final two shots have moved to detailing the full body, with Kylie almost contorted into the inviting poses of the pin-up, simultaneously revealing and concealing. The present persona of a savvy, sexy woman with agency must be mapped from other parts of her celebrity text onto these, cued by the exaggeration in the poses: alone they are insufficiently anchored to let us read her as a person in control.

(a)

(b)

(c)

(d)

Figure 2.5 *Some of Kylie Minogue's album covers: (a)* Kylie *(1988); (b)* Body Language *(2003); (c)* Kylie Minogue *(1994); (d)* Fever *(2001)*

Together the images and the stories about Kylie Minogue not only serve to indicate that personae can modulate (especially when as here, the person grows to adulthood in public), but also demonstrate the intersection of celebrity and changing social values. Actor and singer Judy Garland also had a considerable gay following (see Dyer 1987,

Chapter 3) – an example in Hall's terms (1980) of an oppositional reading of the representations of Garland. In contrast to Kylie's public enjoyment of her gay audience, it was not possible during the 1950s and early 1960s, when homosexual activities were illegal, for any such audience to be acknowledged by the star in her publicity.

The large celebrity text of Kylie Minogue demonstrates how media coverage of a celebrity career not only intersects with social change brought about by gay liberation, but also by feminism and an increase in the prominence of commodity culture. The move to a more commoditised feminism, sometimes called post-feminism (see for example, Kim, 2001) has been particularly important. As far as media representation is concerned, no longer is being sexy and interested in clothes an indication of being incapable of independent decision-making or professional advancement. Instead, there is a heightened valuation of fashion as an industry and as a component of lifestyle decisions. Newspapers carry larger fashion sections or supplements than has previously been the case and do not do so as part of the (devalued) 'women's pages'. Magazines devoted to male fashion have proliferated (see Nixon, 1996) and in both of these the presence of celebrities is substantial. The major media change in the last thirty years has been the considerable increase in the sheer number of celebrities being given media attention, and the almost equally substantial increase in the proportion of commodity promotion that involves celebrities, whether or not these involve their core texts.

5   Celebrities and newsworthiness

As was made clear in Chapter 1, celebrity has become one of the principal ways in which information is disseminated, including information about such apparently different fields as entertainment and politics. Even health advice is provided through stories about celebrities' encounters with illness and their recoveries. For example, on the back of the announcement of Kylie Minogue's breast cancer treatment, the press were full of breast cancer reports and personal stories all of which began with a reference to Kylie. This section will extend this idea that there has been an increase in the way in which the world is textually presented to us through the activities and behaviours of celebrities, by looking at claims about 'tabloidisation'. The term is used to refer to a significant change perceived in the way in which mediated information, in particular news and current affairs, is presented. The term is (obviously) derived from 'tabloid', the smaller-sized, more populist type of newspaper with higher circulations than the more prestigious broadsheets, conventionally seen as important and central to the political process. Before examining the debate about what tabloidisation might involve and why it is relevant here, we shall look at how British tabloids approach stories about celebrities.

Reading 2.3 Activity

Now read the following extract from Ian Connell, 'Personalities in the popular media', (Reading 2.3). Once you have read it through, make some notes on the following questions:

■ What distinction do critics of tabloids set up between human and public interest?

■ How does this tie in to the differences between tabloid and broadsheet newspapers?

■ Why in Connell's view do the tabloids' stories consistently mount attacks on privilege?

Reading 2.3

Ian Connell, 'Personalities in the popular media'

Tabloid stories about personalities do typically provide revelations, exposés of the 'facts' concerning things they have done which they should not have, or which they themselves would prefer not to be widely known. It may be, as I have suggested elsewhere, that their appeal partly arises from this. But this is not all, and not the most important thing, they do. The journalism to be found in the tabloid press is only distantly related to that found in the broadsheets and operates by quite different codes of practice. If broadsheet journalists are primarily concerned with politely reporting and investigating public issues of the moment on ground essentially chosen by the protagonists, the writers of these tabloid stories choose to confront often the same protagonists with themes that they thought safely buried and obscured by their positions in the public domain.

It has often been said of tabloid journalists that their raw material is of 'human' rather than 'public' interest. It is mined from that which ordinary people, remote from the culture's centres of power, have to contend with in their everyday lives. This leads them to deal with themes that are perhaps more persistently problematic features of our cultural formations. I think it is a little more complicated than this suggests. They do deal with matters of 'human interest', why then do so with characters which are drawn from a world so remote from that ordinary world which we might expect to be invoked? Certainly when taken as a whole, there are lots of stories in tabloid papers about 'ordinary people in trouble', but they rarely receive such prominent coverage.

The stories the tabloids tell break the boundaries that have been drawn between that which can and cannot legitimately be discussed in public, by drawing to their readers' attention that which the bearers of public office have deemed private. It is in this sense only that it can be regarded as of 'human' interest. They are rude and raucous intrusions into the sphere of rational public discussion and debate. Their contribution is like someone shouting from somewhere near to, but not at, the centre of the action; 'Stuff the sophisticated arguments, the effete excuses and labyrinthian qualifications – these ba...rds have been caught with their pants down.' (Please feel free to supply adjectives more in keeping with the tabloid styles.) As is often the case with territorial boundaries, these cultural ones are conventional, sometimes imposed, at other times legitimated, but always essentially unstable and, therefore, open to dispute. While there may be no treaties, no lengthy and carefully worded pacts between the parties involved, there have been understandings and 'gentlemen's agreements' governing what can and cannot be written. The tabloid press have found themselves collectively driven to ignore these understandings, perhaps because they have for some time now been engaged in a sharply competitive and costly struggle among themselves. This would not explain, however, why the ground of this struggle has been the deviant doings of the 'great' and good.

Much can be at stake in treating personalities as they do. What we read in the tabloid stories is the yield of a cultural interaction between interests which have become increasingly differentiated and explosive. Depending upon the personalities involved and the nature of the allegations contained in the revelations, the breaches can trigger intense controversy and sometimes costly litigation. Even if the consequent reaction does not go this far, over time the uncontrolled stories have given rise to a generally cautious and disdainful attitude to 'the media' among professional entertainers, other public figures and serious journalists worried, no doubt, about their own standing and credibility. They can be very risky and costly acts for all involved, so we must be curious as to why the tabloid press persist in running them.

Above all what these stories do is mount a populist challenge on privilege. I appreciate this may seem far-fetched. The way I have expressed it makes what goes on in these stories seem far too coherent and calculated. While the stories articulate neither a coherent political philosophy nor strategy, their splenetic outbursts do have, however, important political impact. What these stories do is bash the 'power-bloc' – or those representatives of it whose attributes and actions can be most meaningfully represented for their readers. They give voice to and vent pent-up frustration and indignation at the excesses of those who have come from recognisably ordinary backgrounds, and have 'made it' in understandable ways. [...]

[...]

This [...] raises an interesting proposition about these sorts of stories. The proposition is that not only are they revealing tales, but also tales which set out to teach moral lessons by exposing unworthy and unbecoming actions. Moreover, though perhaps less surprisingly, the moral lessons they teach are relatively simple and conservative ones − of the sort that extra-marital sex is to be avoided. Not for them the complexities of the professional philosopher. Much of what was written about 'Randy Rod', for example, suggests that a major point of narrative interest is whether or not he is capable of living up to the conventional idea of marriage − fidelity. This moralising is not entirely consistent with the other, more common proposition, namely that these papers peddle a prurient interest in sexual matters.

I have said that these stories belong to a hybrid genre that combines elements of fabulous and journalistic writing − fabulous reportage. They are sufficiently driven by journalistic imperatives to take an interest in the disruptive, unexpected or unanticipated. Guaranteed pride of place are stories which deal with just such events in the lives of the rich and famous. Will 'Randy Rod' with his long history of casual affairs really settle down with yet another 'leggy blonde' who is, moreover, his junior by several years? The types of events which are of particular interest to the tabloids can be further specified. They involve actions which are not only unexpected or disruptive, but also unworthy, and unbecoming to a member of the caste of stars or any of the other elevated castes.

[...]

Some final remarks are required on this matter. It does seem to me that fundamentally these stories turn on what are perceived to be abuses of privilege. Their moralising tone adds force, but is dependent on or occasioned by the abuses. The moral condemnation is not the main point of telling the stories. These are political stories, even though their 'structure in dominance' (to indulge in a little old-fashioned structuralist phraseology) is not evidently political. They are political stories inasmuch as (a) they articulate as antagonistic the relations between:

1   powerful elites (from which are drawn the tragic heroes and heroines of the tales);
2   narrators who are by a variety of means in touch with the goings on of the elites, but who are not at one with them;

3   the rest of us, the powerless ordinary people on whose behalf the
     stories are told.

and (b) they focus on the abuses of the rights and privileges that
have been granted the heroes and heroines. I would add two
comments to this. First, these stories do not operate with a
particularly sophisticated political ideology. I have suggested above
that it is a somewhat archaic ideology with respect to its perceptions
of the differences between social strata. Archaic it may be, but we
should not allow this to blind us to the possibility of its continuing
efficacy. It is a political ideology which sees the world divided rather
simply between those who 'have' and those who 'have not'. This
distinction is boldly drawn. The 'haves' have it all – opulent homes,
good-time lifestyles, leggy blondes, big cars and 'inflated' salaries.
They have all the things that the 'have nots' are presumed to desire.
There are even, on occasions, suggestions that they have it all at our
expense.
     [...]
     In a particular light the stories can be read as the expression of
outrage on behalf of the 'have nots'. This can be powerfully and
pleasurably engaging. Why should they have it all? What have they
done to deserve such rewards? What do they know of real work?
What do they care about what happens to the likes of you and me?
Like much populist ranting, however, these stories are quite
conservative. They are not against privileges being granted, merely
angry that they have been granted to the wrong people – to 'them'
and not to 'us', not to 'me'. Their mission is not so much to put a
stop to gross inequalities as to redistribute them. Worse still perhaps
is the possibility that the populism is a sham. The most vitriolic of
the attacks seems to be reserved for those who by good fortune have
found themselves one of the stars. They have not been born to
stardom. It is, therefore, as if the tabloids are waiting for the
inevitable, the moment when these parvenu personalities give
themselves away and reveal the ordinariness of their origins. I do not
wish to sell these stories short, however. While what I have just
suggested can be demonstrated to be true of them, it is also true that
they can and do undermine the authority of those who would place
themselves apart. They encourage and nourish scepticism about the
legitimacy of the class of personalities to act as they do.

Reading source

Connell, 1992, pp.64–83   ■ ■ ■

Connell refers to 'personalities' rather than celebrities, but more importantly he discusses a strikingly different approach to celebrity coverage from that which has been dominant here so far. The term that Connell suggests for the kind of writing in the texts he analyses is 'fabulous reportage' – sadly (in my view) this did not catch on. There are strong links between these kinds of stories and what I have termed 'unauthorised' stories – those based on gossip and candid photographs obtained by means close to 'stalking'. Yet the stories that Connell analyses elsewhere in his article are not from sources like these. The one about 'Randy Rod' Stewart's forthcoming marriage to Rachel Hunter was built up by combining revelations from a ten-year-old autobiography by Stewart's previous wife with illustrations of sexy pictures from Hunter's modelling career and the journalist's moral admonitions. In journalistic terms such stories are 'beat-ups', fabricated out of material produced for other reasons and 're-purposed' to suit the required approach – here the persistent tone of outrage that characterises tabloid exposés of those unjustly privileged. Contrary to my earlier claim that we no longer think of celebrities as more worthy than ordinary people, this tabloid approach is based on the belief that they should be and since they are not, do not deserve what they have.

Despite its importance to a rounded picture of how media texts operate, especially in their representation of celebrities, Connell's 'fabulous reportage' was only a minor component of what came to be termed tabloidisation. In its US inflection, tabloidisation relates particularly to supermarket tabloids, of which the most notorious is the *National Inquirer*, a newspaper which at its height of popularity was obsessed with alien abductions, Elvis sightings and the birth of monsters. John Fiske (1992, p.49) explores the appeal of such stories by noting how, while mainstream media produce a believing subject (the texts' preferred meaning involves being taken to be true), tabloid texts are not interested in this: 'One of [tabloid journalism's] most characteristic tones of voice is that of sceptical laughter which offers the pleasures of disbelief, the pleasures of not being taken in.' The truth of the reporting is not the point; what is important is being party to information in opposition to official knowledge. There are definite continuities with the British tabloids, even if few of them favour alien abduction stories, though *Sunday Sport* did in the 1980s. Some of the disregard for evidence and the more conventional standards of reporting attributed to these papers and the encouragement of scepticism is implicit in most references to tabloidisation, whether in the USA or not.

Not all of the considerable debate about changes in news and current affairs reporting during the mid-1990s referred to the changes as tabloidisation, but they talked about similar things. Bob Franklin (1997, p.4), who can be described as taking a 'cultural decline' perspective (see Chapter 1) used the term 'newszak' to deplore the changes, claiming 'human interest has supplanted the public interest; measured judgement has succumbed to sensationalism; the trivial has triumphed over the weighty; the intimate relationships of celebrities ... are judged more "newsworthy" than the reporting of significant issues and events of international importance.'

Not all critics opposed the new practices (see, for example, those taking a 'populist' view discussed in Chapter 1). Both Catharine Lumby (1997, pp.117–35) and John Hartley (1996, pp.171–95) have discussed tabloidisation of news media, especially its greater proportion of human interest, sex and celebrity, as involving the feminisation of media practices – and done so approvingly. What is important for our purposes here is the centrality of celebrity to the perceived changes. Regardless of the position adopted, the critics all observed an increase in the presence of celebrity in the news media. For those who disliked the changes, this was central to the trivialisation that they detected. One way to start to assess the situation is to ask if the increase really occurred. Such quantitative questions (what is called content analysis) can complement the textual analysis we have engaged in so far. The study of Australian celebrity referred to earlier measured the increase in a sample of print and television news media as well as popular magazines and daytime television chat-shows. That survey, conducted in 1997, found between two and three times more coverage of celebrities in every outlet sampled compared to twenty years earlier (Turner et al., 2000, pp.16–23). Stories about celebrities were displacing what is more customarily considered news content, but it was not clear-cut: analysis of the individual texts revealed that some of the items dealt with news material in what might be considered a *celebritised* way (see Chapter 1; Turner et al., 2000, pp.16–23). Senior politicians' policies could be interwoven with stories about their wives, children and even houses; businessmen's relationships with their mistresses were deemed financially relevant. As you saw in Chapter 1, this has some precedents in early twentieth-century 'human interest' journalism.

Activity 2.8

Find an item in the news that presents a political or business figure in a celebritised way. How separable are the political or business components from the private or promotional ones? ■ ■ ■

Perhaps you noticed how it is often very difficult to separate the aspects out. Richard Branson is one example of a person renowned for integrating his celebrity persona and his business interests.

However much some of the proponents of the tabloidisation debate may have wanted to return the news media to its previous state where a greater proportion of the news was de-personalized and celebrity (much) less prominent, they have not been effective in this desire. Texts about celebrities are popular and entertaining; celebrities are, as the Oxfam study in Chapter 1, Section 4 demonstrated, able to draw attention to serious issues that may not otherwise receive coverage. A significant amount of the mediated information we learn about the world we live in is conveyed in stories that one way or another concern celebrities.

6 Conclusion

As you moved through the various techniques we can use to analyse media texts in Sections 2 to 4, you should have discovered how rich even the simplest text can be in its drawing on political, social and cultural meanings discernible by close attention. Textual analysis enables you to register and negotiate the polysemy of texts and to see how the preferred reading is not the only one available. The preferred reading may be given prominence, however, by anchoring or by the genre chosen. By analysing a number of related texts, it becomes possible to talk about how certain things are represented. For example, the role of celebrities in promoting the consumption of far more than their own products becomes particularly clear as we read magazines looking at red carpet shots or articles about celebrity homes.

While stories about celebrities may appear, and indeed be, trivial at first glance, when you study them systematically they reveal changing social values and beliefs. The case study of Kylie Minogue showed a level of normalisation of homosexuality, as well as the development of a way of seeing both consumption and self-promotion as indicative of female agency.

As you saw in Section 5, celebrities are particularly implicated in the changed contemporary media practice named by the contentious term 'tabloidisation'. The increase in their very presence is enough for some to see a decline in standards of journalism, which tells us also about one way in which celebrity itself is viewed (see Chapter 1). Textual analysis, aided by a quantitative investigation, enables a more nuanced understanding. Celebrity is indeed a major mode through which mediated texts operate, but it has also become a major way through which people apprehend how the world itself operates.

Further reading

deCordova, R. (1990) *Picture Personalities: The Emergence of the Star System in America*, Urbana, IL, University of Illinois Press.

Dyer, R (1998) *Stars* (revised edition), London, BFI Publishing.

Dyer, R. (1987) *Heavenly Bodies: Film Stars and Society*, London, Macmillan.

Neale, S. (1990) 'Questions of genre', *Screen*, vol.31, no.1, pp.45–66.

Neale, S. (2000) *Genre and Hollywood*, London, Routledge.

Thompson, J.B. (1990) *Ideology and Modern Culture: Critical Social Theory in the Era of Mass Communication*, Stanford, CA, Stanford University Press.

Tolson, A. (1996) *Mediations: Text and Discourse in Media Studies*, London, Edward Arnold.

Turner, G., Bonner, F. and Marshall, P.D. (2000) *Fame Games: The Production of Celebrity in Australia*, Cambridge, Cambridge University Press.

References

Barber, L. (1998) *Demon Barber*, London, Viking.

Barthes, R. (1977) *Image–Music–Text* (ed. and trans. S. Heath), London, Fontana.

Bonner, F. (2003) *Ordinary Television*, London, Sage.

Boorstin, D.J. (1961) *The Image: Or What Happened to the American Dream*, Harmondsworth, Penguin.

Connell, I. (1992) 'Personalities in the popular media' in Dahlgren, P. and Sparks, C. (eds) *Journalism and Popular Culture*, London, Sage.

deCordova, R. (1990) *Picture Personalities: The Emergence of the Star System in America*, Urbana, IL, University of Illinois Press.

Dyer, R (1998) *Stars* (revised edition), London, BFI Publishing.

Dyer, R. (1987) *Heavenly Bodies: Film Stars and Society*, London, Macmillan.

Fiske, J. (1987) *Television Culture*, London, Methuen.

Fiske, J. (1992) 'Popularity and the politics of information' in Dahlgren, P. and Sparks, C. (eds) *Journalism and Popular Culture*, London, Sage.

Franklin, B. (1997) *Newszak and News Media*, London, Edward Arnold.

Giles, D. (2000) *Illusions of Immortality: A Psychology of Fame and Celebrity*, New York, St Martin's Press.

Gillespie, M. and Toynbee, J. (eds) (2006) *Analysing Media Texts*, Maidenhead, Open University Press/The Open University (Book 4 in this series).

Hall, S. (1980) 'Encoding/Decoding' in Hall, S., Hobson, D., Lowe, A. and Willis, P. (eds) *Culture, Media, Language*, London, Hutchinson.

Hall, S. (1985) 'Signification, representation, ideology: Althusser and the post-structuralist debates', *Critical Studies in Mass Communication*, vol.2, no.2, pp.91–114.

Hartley, J. (1996) *Popular Reality: Journalism, Modernity, Popular Culture*, London, Edward Arnold.

Horton, D. and Wohl, R. (1993) 'Mass communication and para-social interaction' in Corner, J. and Hawthorne, J. (eds) *Communication Studies: An Introductory Reader*, London, Edward Arnold.

Kim, L.S. (2001) 'Sex and the single girl', *Television and New Media*, vol.2, no.4, pp. 319–34.

Langer, J. (1981) 'Television's "personality" system', *Media, Culture and Society*, vol.3, no.4, pp.351–65.

Lukow, G. and Ricci, S. (1984) 'The "audience" goes "public": intertextuality, genre and the responsibilities of film literacy', *On Film*, vol.12, pp.29–36.

Lumby, C. (1997) *Bad Girls: The Media, Sex and Feminism in the '90s*, Sydney, Allen and Unwin.

Marshall, P.D. (1997) *Celebrity and Power: Fame in Contemporary Culture*, Minneapolis, MN, University of Minnesota Press.

Neale, S. (1980) *Genre*, London, BFI Publishing.

Neale, S. (1990) 'Questions of genre', *Screen*, vol.31, no.1, pp.45–66.

Neale, S. (2000) *Genre and Hollywood*, London, Routledge.

Nixon, S. (1996) *Hard Looks: Masculinities, Spectatorship and Contemporary Consumption*, London, University College of London Press.

Perkins, T.E. (1979) 'Rethinking stereotypes' in Barratt, M., Corrigan, P., Kuhn, A. and Wolff, J. (eds) *Ideology and Cultural Production*, London, Croom Helm.

Sekula, A. (1984) *Photography Against the Grain: Essays and Photo Works 1973–1983*, Halifax, Nova Scotia College of Art and Design.

Tolson, A. (1996) *Mediations: Text and Discourse in Media Studies*, London, Edward Arnold.

Thompson, J.B. (1990) *Ideology and Modern Culture: Critical Social Theory in the Era of Mass Communication*, Stanford, CA, Stanford University Press.

Turner, G., Bonner, F. and Marshall, P.D. (2000) *Fame Games: The Production of Celebrity in Australia*, Cambridge, Cambridge University Press.

Vincent, S. (2003) 'Pretty boys can think', *The Guardian*, 15 February, p.18.

Plate 1
(see Activity 1.1, Chapter 1)

Plate 2 *Classic Soul* (a)
(see Activity 3.2, Chapter 3)

Plate 3 *Son of Redneck* (a)
(see Activity 3.2, Chapter 3)

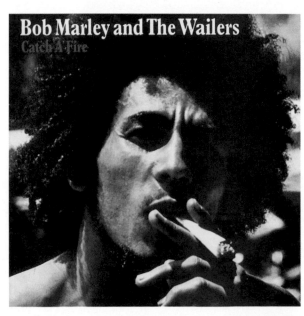

Plate 4 Bob Marley and the Wailers, *Catch a Fire* (b)
(see Activity 3.2, Chapter 3)

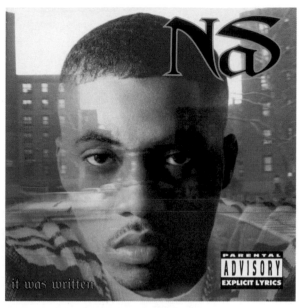

Plate 5 NaS, *It was Written* (b)
(see Activity 3.2, Chapter 3)

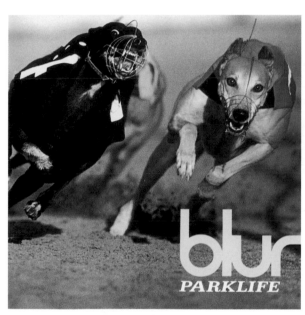

Plate 6 Blur, *Parklife* – front cover (b)
(see Activity 3.2, Chapter 3)

Plate 7 Blur, *Parklife* – back cover (b)
(see Activity 3.2, Chapter 3)

Plate 8 *National Enquirer* magazine
(see Section 4.2, Chapter 3)

'And We're Going to Go to Trial'

Interview: 'I've been through Oklahoma City'

TIMOTHY McVEIGH AND HIS LAWYER, Stephen Jones, met for an exclusive interview last week in El Reno Federal Correctional Institution with NEWSWEEK's Col. David H. Hackworth and Peter Annin. Over 70 minutes, they discussed McVeigh's past, his life in the military — and the Oklahoma City bombing. Excerpts:

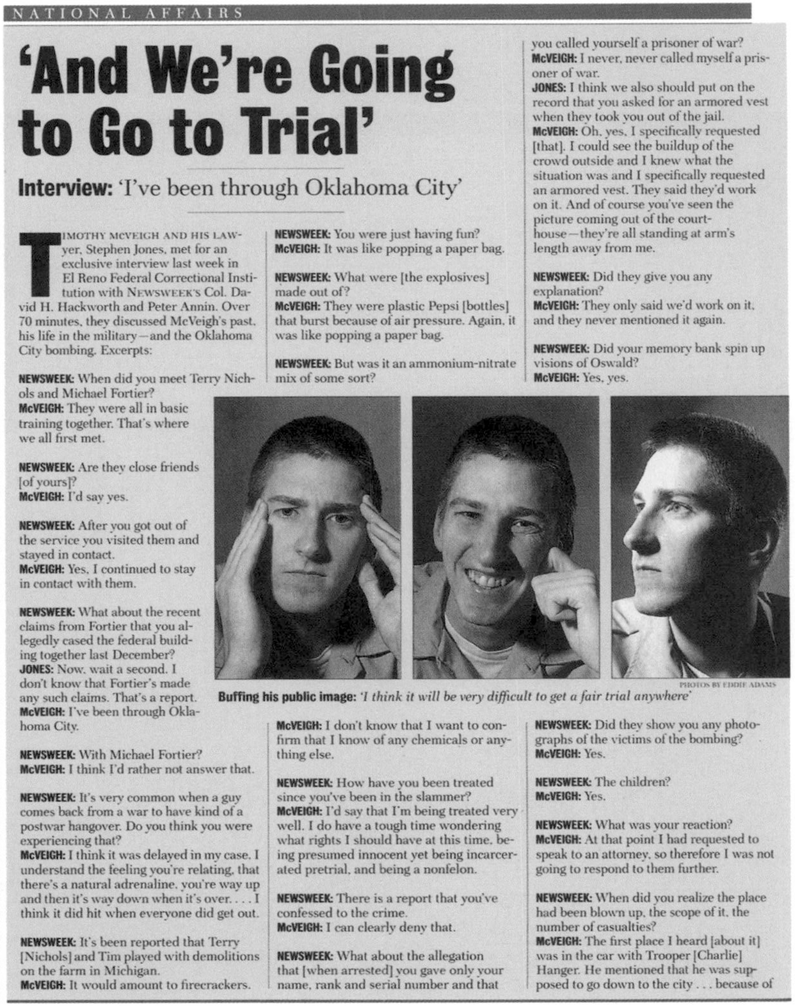

NEWSWEEK: When did you meet Terry Nichols and Michael Fortier?
McVEIGH: They were all in basic training together. That's where we all first met.

NEWSWEEK: Are they close friends [of yours]?
McVEIGH: I'd say yes.

NEWSWEEK: After you got out of the service you visited them and stayed in contact.
McVEIGH: Yes, I continued to stay in contact with them.

NEWSWEEK: What about the recent claims from Fortier that you allegedly cased the federal building together last December?
JONES: Now, wait a second. I don't know that Fortier's made any such claims. That's a report.
McVEIGH: I've been through Oklahoma City.

NEWSWEEK: With Michael Fortier?
McVEIGH: I think I'd rather not answer that.

NEWSWEEK: It's very common when a guy comes back from a war to have kind of a postwar hangover. Do you think you were experiencing that?
McVEIGH: I think it was delayed in my case. I understand the feeling you're relating, that there's a natural adrenaline, you're way up and then it's way down when it's over. . . . I think it did hit when everyone did get out.

NEWSWEEK: It's been reported that Terry [Nichols] and Tim played with demolitions on the farm in Michigan.
McVEIGH: It would amount to firecrackers.

NEWSWEEK: You were just having fun?
McVEIGH: It was like popping a paper bag.

NEWSWEEK: What were [the explosives] made out of?
McVEIGH: They were plastic Pepsi [bottles] that burst because of air pressure. Again, it was like popping a paper bag.

NEWSWEEK: But was it an ammonium-nitrate mix of some sort?

PHOTOS BY EDDIE ADAMS

Buffing his public image: *'I think it will be very difficult to get a fair trial anywhere'*

McVEIGH: I don't know that I want to confirm that I know of any chemicals or anything else.

NEWSWEEK: How have you been treated since you've been in the slammer?
McVEIGH: I'd say that I'm being treated very well. I do have a tough time wondering what rights I should have at this time, because being presumed innocent yet being incarcerated pretrial, and being a nonfelon.

NEWSWEEK: There is a report that you've confessed to the crime.
McVEIGH: I can clearly deny that.

NEWSWEEK: What about the allegation that [when arrested] you gave only your name, rank and serial number and that

you called yourself a prisoner of war?
McVEIGH: I never, never called myself a prisoner of war.
JONES: I think we also should put on the record that you asked for an armored vest when they took you out of the jail.
McVEIGH: Oh, yes. I specifically requested [that]. I could see the buildup of the crowd outside and I knew what the situation was and I specifically requested an armored vest. They said they'd work on it. And of course you've seen the picture coming out of the courthouse—they're all standing at arm's length away from me.

NEWSWEEK: Did they give you any explanation?
McVEIGH: They only said we'd work on it, and they never mentioned it again.

NEWSWEEK: Did your memory bank spin up visions of Oswald?
McVEIGH: Yes, yes.

NEWSWEEK: Did they show you any photographs of the victims of the bombing?
McVEIGH: Yes.

NEWSWEEK: The children?
McVEIGH: Yes.

NEWSWEEK: What was your reaction?
McVEIGH: At that point I had requested to speak to an attorney, so therefore I was not going to respond to them further.

NEWSWEEK: When did you realize the place had been blown up, the scope of it, the number of casualties?
McVEIGH: The first place I heard [about it] was in the car with Trooper [Charlie] Hanger. He mentioned that he was supposed to go down to the city . . . because of

Plate 10 Newsweek inside spread, July 3, 1995
(see Activity 1.1, Chapter 1)

Newsweek

July 3, 1995 · $2.95

EXCLUSIVE

The Suspect Speaks

A Prison Interview With Alleged Oklahoma City Bomber Timothy McVeigh

Plate 9 Newsweek front cover, July 3, 1995, showing Timothy McVeigh, convicted of Oklahoma bombing
(see Activity 1.1, Chapter 1)

CLAIRE GOOSE

THE TV STAR'S PERSONAL DIARY OF HER VISIT TO ETHIOPIA TO MEET THE COFFEE FARMERS WHO ARE FACING TRAGEDY

"Coffee is killing us," says 35-year-old Marolla, clasping British actress Claire Goose by the hand and asking people to take responsibility for what is in their coffee cup. The bottom line is that if farmers don't get a fair price for their coffee they will starve.

Marolla appeals to Claire to take her message home: it is a cry for help from the starving coffee farmers in Ethiopia to the millions of coffee drinkers in the UK.

This is Claire's much-deserved week off after two months filming the third series of BBC hit drama *Waking The Dead*. But rather than put her feet up at home, she has come with Oxfam on a six-day trip to visit the Kafa region of Ethiopia – the birthplace of coffee – and see for herself the devastating effects that a world slump in coffee prices is having on the farmers who produce it.

Ethiopia, already one of the poorest countries in the world, is now in the grips of a drought which is threatening a terrible famine. Last week, *Live Aid* founder Sir Bob Geldof warned that Ethiopia may be facing an even greater food crisis than the one which devastated the country in the 1980s.

So far, the coffee-growing region, which is comparatively lush, has escaped famine. However, with the drop in income for the country's vital coffee exports, Ethiopia is staring at yet another awful humanitarian crisis.

Claire, who arrives at Heathrow exhausted after a week of nightmare shoots, seems nervous about her responsibility. 'This isn't like the trip I did with the Red Cross to the flooded areas of Mozambique,'

where we were asking for money,' the actress says. 'This is about shifting habits and getting people to take responsibility for what is in their coffee cup. And it is that if farmers don't get a fair price for their coffee they'll starve.'

The former *Casualty* actress, one of Britain's most popular TV stars, is not at all fazed by the basic facilities she encounters in Ethiopia. While Claire admits that she enjoys all the comforts that celebrity brings, she equally hankers after a simple life. She isn't a slave to designer labels and prefers weekends with her parents in Norfolk to going clubbing in London. After ending her four-year relationship with fellow *Casualty* actor Jonathan Kerrigan last year, she is also happily single: "Although I'm sure once I meet the right person I'll have no qualms about settling down," she says.

In Ethiopia, Claire is as passionate about helping the individual coffee farmers as she is about bringing their message home. One of her immediate aims when she returns is to set up a meeting with Tony Blair in order to open his eyes to the grim facts of the coffee crisis.

Here, Claire writes a personal diary for *HELLO!* about her moving visit to Ethiopia and tells how the charity mission has helped the actress put her career and relationship breakup into perspective.

Day One

I've come from such a manic filming schedule that

Claire stops en route to the coffee district to chat to a passerby (below). 'I love seeing how people walk everywhere,' she says. 'Transport is a huge issue here and suddenly being chauffeur-driven on to set every day seems an obscene luxury.' The actress meets the children of coffee farmers (right)

I can't get my head round coffee yet. Last night I finished shooting at two in the morning, rushed home to grab a few hours' kip, then scooped up my stuff to get to Heathrow in time.

I'm too keyed up to sleep on the nine-hour flight so arrive exhausted at Addis Ababa at three in the morning. We book into a hotel but I don't sleep a wink because of the traffic. Then we climb into a jeep for another eight-hour bone-shaker of a ride to the southwest coffee region of Kafa.

I'm so disorientated. I'm aware I'm not being very sociable but I'm trying to get my head round the issue. It's not a case of ranting and raving, it's about getting people to understand that the quality coffee grown by the 1.2 million Ethiopian farmers will cease to exist if consumers like me don't start buying fair trade coffee back home.

Since coffee accounts for about 60 per cent of Ethiopia's exports it's more than just farmers starving – everyone will suffer. And it's a similar picture for coffee producers all over the world.

Day Two

We're staying in Jimma – once the thriving capital of the coffee region but fast becoming a sleepy poverty-stricken backwater. This is one of the lushest areas of Ethiopia where up until now people have been spared famine.

I sleep badly, up twice – the second time to take my malaria tablets. I'm no longer unbearably tired but I'm still not my normal chatty self. Usually it takes a lot to shut me up.

First stop is Haro co-operative where farmers get a better price for their coffee by cutting out the middle men. The chief man proudly points out all the trophies and certificates they've won for their quality coffee, but laments these desperate times with coffee prices plummeting to an all-time low.

The only hope, he says, is if the big companies start to pay a fair price for coffee. While I'm sitting in the hot cramped room I suddenly feel as if I'm having a panic attack. It's as if people are talking double-speak and I have to get out. Perhaps it's the malaria tablets because I'm not nervous.

The first attack I ever had was shortly after I split up with Jon. I was shopping in Richmond and suddenly this anxiety just gripped me and I had to get home. The next time was at a premiere. Now I can rationalise myself out of them by breathing and focusing on something.

I love knowing how things work so it's been great seeing how the red coffee beans are picked from the trees and then weighed, graded, washed and dried. Talking to two women farmers – Marolla and Mikka – brings it all home. They tell me that they can't clothe or feed their children let alone afford to send them to school. There are days they go without food altogether. Marolla says she will give coffee another two years but if the price doesn't go up she'll have no choice but to cut down her coffee trees and grow just enough maize to feed her family instead. Like that, she may survive, she says.

If nothing is done the farmers will lose everything. What we at home just don't get is that some big companies have been increasingly diluting and blending the quality coffee of Ethiopia

with cheap coffees from countries like Brazil and Vietnam. It's a clever marketing trick which is slowly altering our taste. So while the labelling gets more and more sophisticated, the coffee we drink is increasingly impure and inferior.

Day Three

We are invited to a coffee ceremony in a family's mud and straw home. Three times a day, several families gather to drink coffee and pray to bless the land and increase the price of coffee.

I'm not a regular churchgoer but I have a spiritual side and I love the way they give thanks for the little they have. I like the pace of life here. Like at home there's no rush so you have time to sit down, be alone have coffee with my neighbours.

What is so impressive here is that people still try to help each other although they are at pre-starvation levels. It seems to take a tragedy like Soham back home for a whole community to unite. What I also improve is that no one here has asked for money, all they want is for us to tell their story to the outside world.

governments – don't do something.

Before leaving I meet Birkisa – she is a 28-year-old single mum who still wants to complete her schooling because only then is there hope for a better life. Her main concern is for her community. "If things don't improve, children won't go to school and everyone will concentrate around the village," she says. "There will be no work, more crime and the community will perish."

I feel uncomfortable meeting someone so briefly and then walking away, especially when they are so grateful. I feel guilty, too, that at home I can get so absorbed in my own little troubles which seem so trivial by comparison.

We drive back to Addis Ababa. I keep thinking of solutions. The simple answer is to buy fair trade coffee because that ensures the farmer gets a fair price. Oxfam is lobbying the big companies to commit to purchasing two per cent of their coffee under fair trade conditions. It's pathetic that they won't even do that yet. ▶

143

Plate 11a & 11b Claire Goose's personal diary of her visit to Ethiopia. Page spread from *Hello!* magazine
(see Activity 1.5, Chapter 1)

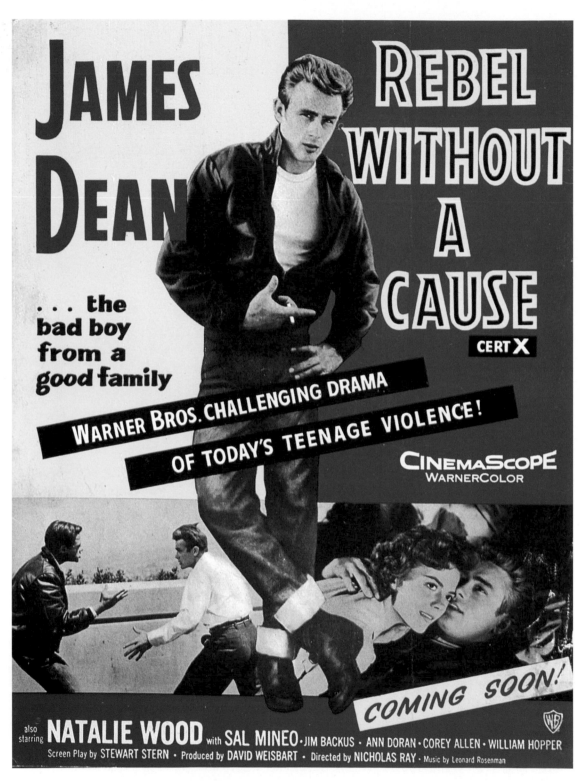

Plate 12 *Rebel Without a Cause* (1955)
(see Section 2.2, Chapter 4)

Producing celebrity

Chapter 3

David Hesmondhalgh

Contents

1 Three approaches to media production and celebrity

The primary aim of this chapter is to examine how we might understand the phenomenon of celebrity by looking at the institutions of media production. But we cannot do this by simply explaining 'how media production works'. A number of different ways of understanding media production exist, and so the second aim of the chapter is to introduce and explain some of these different, often competing, approaches and to consider their relative advantages and disadvantages. We shall compare three approaches to the study of media production, by examining the way in which they understand the phenomenon of celebrity.

The first, an organisational approach, emphasises the internal dynamics of the institutions involved in the production and marketing of celebrities. The second, a political economy approach, is much more concerned with the imperatives driving media companies as profit-making businesses, how this affects what such companies produce, and what this says about the role of media production in societies. The third approach, inspired by the work of post-structuralists such as the French historian Michel Foucault, holds media industries responsible for the production of certain kinds of relationships between celebrities and audiences, which in turn have an effect on key aspects of modern societies. (These approaches are summarised in Table 3.1, in the final section of this chapter, and you can use this table to help follow my account.)

All the approaches we will examine in this chapter show that fame is not something that just happens randomly, or as a result of individual talent or charisma, which is how the media themselves tend to present fame; rather it is socially produced. This underlines an important point in the book as a whole (see Book Introduction), as it shows how studies of the media can reveal that processes that seem simple and commonsensical are actually the product of complex social forces. In addition, the approaches embody different attitudes to questions concerning the power of the media.

2 An organisational approach: the everyday shaping of celebrity

The first approach to celebrity and media production can be labelled as the *sociology of media organisations*. This type of research involves the detailed study of the way in which media professionals go about, and conceive of, their work and how their conceptions and practices affect media products. The organisational approach takes great interest in the empirical details of everyday life behind the scenes of media production. Because of this attention to the *micro* level, there tends to be less space for those following this approach to focus on the *macro* level – on social systems and structures. The sociology of media organisations might also be accused of being somewhat *empiricist* in its orientation, rather than merely *empirical*. The term 'empiricist', when used negatively, refers to research that prioritises the collection and presentation of observational and other data at the expense of the development of *theories*. However, empirical work – interviewing, observing, gathering statistics – is not necessarily empiricist and should ideally help to generate better theories about, say, the media, or about celebrity. Research that begins as empirical work can become empiricist when it becomes cut off from the wider goal of generating explanations and evaluations of what happens in the world. While empiricism is a danger of a sociology that is concerned with the fine detail of the micro, an empirical approach also offers rich potential. The organisational sociology approach can be particularly effective in showing that celebrity is constructed and produced within particular institutional contexts. It can show in detail how celebrity is actively constructed by various groups of people with different interests.

The US sociologist Joshua Gamson provides a good example of this approach to the production of celebrity in his book *Claims to Fame: Celebrity in Contemporary America*. He offers a detailed account of the workings of the celebrity-making industry in Los Angeles. The emphasis is on the everyday shaping of celebrity. A remarkably complex division of labour surrounds celebrities. Perhaps most notable are the personal publicists and PR companies who, in Gamson's words, 'handle the garnering of media coverage' (Gamson, 1994, p.55). Agents, managers and promoters work as representatives of aspiring or actual stars, negotiating deals and working with publicists on the project of moulding and reshaping the star persona. Celebrities, Gamson shows, are at the centre of a circle of coaches and groomers who cut their hair, train their bodies in the gym, teach them how to speak better, move better, eat better. He identifies four main groups who can make a profit from the successful fostering of a celebrity:

- the various individuals and companies involved in the production of celebrity, who are hired by the aspiring or actual celebrities to mould their persona
- entertainment institutions, such as film and television companies, which use the celebrity to market their product
- the news and entertainment media (newspapers, magazines, television, radio and now the internet), which use celebrities to fill space and air-time, but also to sell publications or build up audience ratings

> ■ ancillary industries, such as tourist companies, which arrange trips to see the homes of celebrities.

These different groups have different interests, but they are tightly linked in social networks, meeting at parties and premières and exchanging 'a continuous and voluminous flow of letters, faxes and phone calls' (Gamson, 1994, p.65). Gamson's account reveals how the production of celebrity in Los Angeles involved a particular set of shared understandings about how to operate. A term increasingly used for producers' shared understandings of workplaces and other institutions is 'culture'. So some recent analysts have written about the need to study not only the production of culture (in our case, the production of media celebrity) and how culture comes to us, but also 'cultures of production' (Negus, 1997): that is, the values, meanings and working practices that inform such production. Gamson demonstrates the usefulness of such an approach.

Gamson's study also demonstrates how approaches to an area of study such as media production tend to carry with them particular sets of research *methods*. The sociology of media organisations has drawn mainly on three methods: participant observation (a method where the researcher spends considerable time in the community or institution s/he is reporting upon); the examination of professional documents of various kinds; and interviews with media workers. We will not explore participant observation here (but see **Hesmondhalgh, 2006**). However, adopting the role of organisational sociologists, we will look at a professional document in the form of an extract from a marketing textbook (Reading 3.1) and will see how it attempts to guide media workers and trainees in how to publicise celebrities. The authors of the marketing textbook do this by analysing a celebrity biography (which is a form of publicity) to bring out what they think are the most compelling elements of stories about celebrities. We then examine an ordinary newspaper story about a celebrity (Reading 3.2) in order to see how similar ideas about what makes for a compelling story operate amongst media workers – even though they are unlikely to have read the particular textbook in Reading 3.1. This shows how shared values and beliefs operate amongst media workers in the production of celebrity. Then, again adopting the role of organisational sociologists, we will read extracts from interviews with media workers (Reading 3.3), conducted by Gamson, in order to consider the potential usefulness of research interviews for understanding media production.

2.1 Looking at the output of media workers

In Reading 3.1, Rein et al. discuss a biography of US evangelist, Robert Schuller (see Figure 3.1).

Reading 3.1 Activity

Now read the following extract from Irving Rein, Philip Kotler and Martin Stoller, 'Marketing celebrities: elements of dramatic reality' (Reading 3.1). This is taken from *High Visibility*, a textbook for marketers about the marketing of celebrities. Make notes of the main elements that the authors consider are present in celebrity publicity stories.

Reading 3.1

Irving Rein, Philip Kotler and Martin Stoller, 'Marketing celebrities: elements of dramatic reality'

In the best-selling biography *Robert Schuller: The Inside Story* the story is told of the celebrity evangelist's trip into the unknown as a newly ordained minister heading to the promised land of California:

> There was snow on the ground that February day as Bob and Arvella Schuller loaded their old Chevrolet with their few meager belongings and lovingly tucked three-year-old Sheila and baby Bobby into the back seat. Their breath hung in puffs of steam as they carried their things from their little parsonage. This was it. There would be no turning back now ...
>
> Just before their departure, a denominational representative had phoned him to say that there were simply no halls to rent for their new church ...
>
> 'There's bound to be some place where we can hold services for the church,' Bob determined. 'I know it can't be impossible.' Without another word, he grabbed a white paper napkin from the table, pulled a pen from his pocket, and began to write ...
>
> Nason and Nason, 1981, pp.45–6

It's a wonderful story. Is it true? Does it matter? The point is that it is a compelling story, imbuing Schuller and his quest with high drama. The audience sees itself in Schuller's shoes – on a mission, alone, facing the unknown. There is mystery: What did Schuller write? There is suspense: Where

Figure 3.1 Robert Schuller, US evangelist

would he find a church? It's a perfect illustration of how dramatic reality is one of the most potent of the celebrity-audience attachment strategies. Yet, it is also one of the least well utilized and understood. Clearly, certain combinations of stories and character types can draw audiences into deep involvement with celebrities. But although we know that stories have lesson-giving power, often serving as models of behavior, little analysis has been devoted to understanding what makes them work.

Examining stories for their persuasive power, it is possible to identify their key components, to help achieve the best match between story and aspirant. To begin, most celebrity stories contain a mixture of six major elements:

- Drama: a beginning, middle, and end revolving around some sort of conflict.
- Adversity: a roadblock that has to be overcome.
- Crisis: sickness, drugs, divorce, an event that brings the adversity into focus.
- Mentors: trainers, advisers, parents, or agents who provide some form of guidance.
- Unrelenting talent: some skill that simply must be used or understood.
- A final reward or climax: public acclamation, a huge audience, charity work, or even a noble death.

In Schuller's case, the elements virtually leap out of the story:

The Drama: the search for a place to preach, his eventual selection of the last possibility Schuller had written on that fateful napkin – a drive-in movie theater.

The Crisis: his poverty and inexperience, the absence of parishioners ('His self-confidence was shattered, he had already spent all the money, the advertisements had run.')

The Adversity: the local clergy's opposition to his preaching in a drive-in ('One pastor came over eight days before the opening service and proceeded to lambast Bob for holding services in a "passion pit".')

The Mentors: the 'heroic' support of Dr. Norman Vincent Peale ('Bob admits to grabbing onto Norman's coattails.')

The Unrelenting Talent: Schuller's 'booming theatrical preaching style'.

The Final Reward: worldwide celebrity, culminating in the construction of the Crystal Cathedral.

Interwoven, the six elements in Schuller's story form several classic themes or story lines.

[...]

When trying to match aspirants to the most useful story lines, some generalizations can be drawn:

- Certain aspirants are more fitted to play the roles necessary to bring certain kernel stories to life.
- Few celebrities use only one story; many different stories are used over time to appeal to different audiences.
- With the media transmitting more images – of clothes, faces, walks, hairstyles –marketers are able to tell and reinforce a story more effectively.
- With the decline of traditional family units and communities, we are relying more on celebrities – not grandparents and neighbors –to embody, make real, and transmit our stories and moral tales.

The key is story control. The celebrity and his or her developers seize the initiative—selecting the story, refining it, and managing its distribution. Is the story appropriate to the sector and aspirant? Is it memorable? Can it be widely distributed? Are the channels efficiently used? Are relations with the press exploited? These are the questions that the successful exploiters of stories ask. If they don't, someone else –the unfriendly media, the professional muckraker – may do it instead, with far less favorable results.

Reference

Nason, M. and Nason, D. (1981) *Robert Schuller: The Inside Story*, Wheaton, Ill., TyndaleHouse.

Reading source

Rein et al., 1997, pp.142–6 ■ ■ ■

It is important to realise that, in our adopted role as organisational sociologists, we are not examining this piece in order to gain knowledge about how celebrities might be most efficiently marketed. The aim is to discern the values that are at work in such marketing. This can help us to understand how media texts come to take the form they do. To test this, let us look at an ordinary, everyday piece of celebrity journalism.

Reading 3.2 Activity

In order to see how the elements identified by Rein et al. might work in a piece of celebrity journalism, read the following extracts from Clare Donnelly, 'I was a *Full Monty* star...' (Reading 3.2), from the British newspaper, the *Daily Mirror* (see Figure 3.2). Make notes on these questions:

- Can you identify which of the strategies identified by Rein, Kotler and Stoller are being used here?
- Besides the 'celebrity' himself, what other product does this piece serve to promote?

Reading 3.2

Claire Donnelly, 'I was a *Full Monty* star ... then a road accident sent my world crashing'

Exclusive: how *Emmerdale*'s William rebuilt his dreams of fame

As the child star of hit film *The Full Monty*, William Snape seemed set for a long and glittering showbiz career. At 12, he caused a sensation in the Oscar-nominated movie and was bombarded, by directors believing he was the next big thing. Between auditions, William spent his time being mobbed by fans and enjoying the celebrity circuit.

But the bubble burst for the Sheffield-born schoolboy as he struggled to get his next big break. William – known to friends and family as Wim – was involved in a horrific accident. His family feared he would die and doctors were amazed he did not lose his leg. Now 17, he is hoping to make his mark again after joining ITV soap *Emmerdale* as farmer Stephen Butler.

Speaking of his ordeal for the first time, he reveals the truth about his accident and tells how his faltering career left him depressed and disheartened.

[...]

Lady Luck has certainly been a fickle mistress to William. Plucked from obscurity to play Nathan, Robert Carlyle's son in the 1997 film *The Full Monty*, the Sheffield-born youngster found him self catapulted into the spotlight. 'It all happened very quickly', he says. 'One minute I was at school, the next I was in Hollywood.

[...]

'I went through seven auditions and the last one was nerve-racking because Robert Carlyle was there.

'But we got on and felt really comfortable with each other.' Amazed he got the part – 'when my mum and dad told me, I ran round screaming' – he loved every minute of filming. 'I decided then that I wanted to be an actor,' he says. 'I just knew this was the life for me.' [...]

William flew to LA for the premiere and was inundated with offers. 'There was an after-show party and every actor had their own table and at each there was a queue of about 15 agents, casting directors and managers wanting to sign us up. It was mad.'

Back in England, William who lives with Dad Duncan, 50, and a stepbrother and sister, found himself thrown into the showbiz world 'I enjoyed it all' he says. 'It was overwhelming... At the comedy awards, I remember standing at the urinals with Ewan McGregor and Chris Evans. It was like another world.'

The film made William a rich boy, too. Producer Uberto Pasolini gave the cast and crew a share of the profits, estimated at £100,000 each.

But away from the hype and applause, things weren't so much fun. Some of his friends at Dobcrott Junior School resented William's success and when he moved up to Silverdale School, things got worse.

'At first, I tried not to tell people too much about the filming but it was hard explaining where I'd been for six weeks. It's strange because you soon know who your friends are – a lot of the people I auditioned with were my friends from school ... and they're not now. No one said anything to my face but people would keep their distance.

'For the Year Six ball – at the end of primary school – I hired a limo for all my friends, thinking it would be a laugh. I wasn't trying to be flash; I just thought it would be fun. But my mum told me that some girls were saying: 'Look at him, coming to a little party in a car like that, he's such a show-off.'

[...]

Still trying out for parts – 'It became a routine: audition for something, then get the rejection' – William began to wonder if he'd ever make it. Then at 14, the accident happened and everything changed.

Leaving school one afternoon, he was hit by a car as he crossed the road. His leg was so badly broken, William needed two operations and 18 steel pins to get him back on his feet. Fidgeting nervously, he says: 'One minute I was walking out, the next thing I knew I was flying through the air. I remember seeing red and landing on my head. I was in a lot of pain. I spoke to people later who saw it happen – they said I'd flown so high up, it looked like something out of a film.

[...]

'It was a nightmare really. It's not the type of thing you ever think could happen to you. It was awful for my parents. [...] After things stabilized I had to learn to walk again and needed physiotherapy every day. But I got there in the end.' Still keen to pursue his acting career, William enrolled on a drama course in Chesterfield, Derbyshire, before starting a full-time course in October last year.

But just two months later, he got the big break he'd been waiting for. Trying out for the part of *Emmerdale*'s Stephen Butler, he approached the audition in Leeds with some scepticism. But by the time he got back to Sheffield they'd offered him the job. His first scenes were aired in January and William has since become a regular on the show. He now gets stacks of fan mail, though he's currently single, and says he couldn't be happier – especially because few people recognize him on the street any more.

Dressed in faded jeans and a white Lacoste T-shirt, William looks like any other Yorkshire lad – the only sign of his TV star status is the expensive-looking Burberry bag he slings over his shoulder as he gets ready to leave.

Smiling broadly, he seems to have finally found the success he deserves. 'Everyone has been so kind to me', he explains, 'The cast are great and have made me really welcome – they are some of my best friends now. I'm just pleased that I've been given this chance.

'Acting is a tough business – I've learnt that the hard way – but I feel like things are working out for me.'

Reading source

Daily Mirror, 19 March 2003, p.29 ■ ■ ■

The elements identified by Rein et al. do seem to emerge from this story. As in most news stories, there is an attempt to create *drama*: William is plucked from obscurity, suffers, but wins through. The article focuses in some detail on the *adversity* William faces, including the animosity of other schoolchildren, a car accident and a period out of work. This produces a *crisis* (the 'nightmare'), which is resolved by passing an audition for a prime-time soap (implying *talent*). There are references to the *mentoring* role of co-star Robert Carlyle and the *Emmerdale* cast. The final *reward* is of course 'the success he deserves'.

As you will probably have noticed, the article serves to promote not only William, but also the soap *Emmerdale*. The piece will have been arranged by the publicity department (or press office) of *Emmerdale* based

Figure 3.2 'I was a Full Monty star ...' How the article on William Snape appeared in the Daily Mirror, 19 March 2003

at the offices of Yorkshire Television in Leeds, England, where the programme is produced. Someone in the press office will have contacted a journalist at the *Daily Mirror* and will have suggested that the *Daily Mirror*'s readership would be interested in a piece featuring a member of the cast of the international hit film *The Full Monty*. The article benefits the *Daily Mirror*, because it will be of interest to the millions of people who watched *The Full Monty* and to those who watch *Emmerdale*, and it will benefit the programme makers, because it implies that *Emmerdale* is popular enough to be newsworthy in itself, and it portrays the cast as friendly, supportive, talented and resilient. Of course the article benefits William Snape too by raising his public profile (see Figure 3.3). The close fit between Rein et al.'s typology and the narrative strategies used here doesn't mean that the *Emmerdale* publicity people or the *Daily Mirror* journalists have read such marketing textbooks. Rather, the marketing textbook identifies what journalists tend, by convention and often unconsciously, to put into such stories.

Figure 3.3 *William Snape with Robert Carlyle in the film,* The Full Monty

What does our examination of Readings 3.1 and 3.2 tell us about the organisational sociology approach to media production? Adopting the role of organisational sociologists, we were able to look at professional documents (Reading 3.1) and at the everyday output of media workers (Reading 3.2), in order to gain insights into the kinds of shared values and understandings that are at work in the media industries (in this case, amongst publicists, journalists and celebrities). Using such an organisational approach can be very helpful in showing the complex and co-ordinated nature of much social action, and for thinking about the way in which the social world – including, in this case, knowledge of a particular celebrity – is constructed for certain ends.

2.2 Research interviews with media professionals

Another potentially valuable source of information about media production comes from research interviews with media workers, and the usefulness of this method can also be seen in Joshua Gamson's book. In carrying out and analysing such interviews, we need to be wary of taking what interviewees say at 'face value'. Interviewees may well be guarded, fearing that if they reveal too much about their motives and techniques they will be open to criticism. Or they may simply be reflecting the received wisdom of people in their line of work about what they do, rather than being fully aware of the pressures and constraints they face. Nevertheless, such research interviews can provide very revealing insights into the way in which media workers talk and think.

Reading 3.3 Activity

Now read the following extract from Gamson's book, *Claims to Fame* (Reading 3.3). These are quotations from media workers interviewed by Gamson. Each represents one of the groups identified by Gamson (see the beginning of Section 2). Read these interview extracts and answer the following questions:

- What do each of these quotations suggest, in your view, about the conflicts and collaborations involved in the production of celebrity?
- What images were being sought by the publicists for their celebrities in each case?

Reading 3.3

Joshua Gamson, 'The negotiated celebration'

[A TV producer] A couple of weeks ago we were going after a big star in a big movie. I thought automatically he would do an interview. I was told, 'Well, he's going through a different publicity phase on this.' Between the lines, it was 'He's going to try to take the high road on this,' go for the cover of *Vanity Fair* or *Rolling Stone* rather than *Entertainment Tonight*. I was told he wasn't going to do a lot of other things. In the meantime we were offered three other co-stars from that film, and we did them, and arranged to do the premiere and all that stuff. Then when it came time to start running them, this actor suddenly started showing up on our competition, on *Oprah*, *Donahue*, the morning shows. So I was told by my producers, 'Tell them we're not running any of the stuff we've done unless he agrees to do an interview.' I told the studio and the personal publicist. I was accused of blackmail. It wasn't blackmail, because it was one thing when it started and then all of a sudden the rules changed. So the publicist went to the star, and the star said, 'No way,' got really mad. So we pulled out of covering the premiere that night. It was a big deal. A day and a half later he agreed to do an interview, and he couldn't have been nicer during the interview. So we aired two pieces, and we reinstated our other ones.

[...]

Jordan Kaminsky [A personal publicist], tells of a client who was asked by a syndicated columnist why he went into acting:

He said, 'Because there were a lot of pretty girls I wanted to fuck.' My mouth fell open and I kicked him under the table. I thought, what a fucking idiot. It made him seem like an idiot, like he wasn't serious about acting. What he should have said was, whether it was true or not, was 'I watched Marlon Brando when I was a child and he was so amazing in *On the Waterfront*.' He needed an answer like that. Luckily, I had a relationship with this journalist. I said, 'Do me a favour, either don't use it or at least tone it down,' which he did.

[...]

[A magazine editor] When we assigned a staff writer to do a profile of Candice Bergen, PMK [Bergen's publicity firm] said, 'While we respect this writer we don't think that she would appreciate Candice Bergen's sense of humor.' The persona they were trying to create for Candice Bergen was that she was funny, and they didn't think this particular writer would do their bidding on that. The editors basically said. 'Screw you. If you want to pick your writers, why don't you start your own magazine?' The epilogue is that shortly after this [a new owner] took over, the editor who said fuck you to PMK was fired, and the new people said, 'Okay, who do you want for the piece?'

Reading source

Gamson, 1994, pp.88–90 ■ ■ ■

Gamson uses these quotations to show that the marketing of celebrities is not nearly as neat and easy as marketing textbooks such as *High Visibility* (Reading 3.1) suggest, and that the management of publicity involves great conflict and competition between the different groups. The first quotation shows how the entertainment-news media, on the one hand, and celebrities and their team, on the other, are involved in conflicts and negotiations over access and control. The TV producer, in competition with other TV shows, used the weapon of a threat to discard all publicity for the new film. The publicist in this first story had to persuade the star to give an interview to this low-prestige, high-viewership television show – *Entertainment Tonight* – in order for the publicity work (the interviews with three lesser stars) to be used. The second quotation raises important questions about the ways in which journalists are co-opted by publicity organisations. The journalist agreed to leave out a potentially damaging story as a 'favour' – presumably so that she or he could persuade the publicist and/or celebrity to give him or her privileged access to some future story. The third extract is quoted by Gamson in the context of the following comment: 'In recent years, both publicists and journalists commonly note, the balance of power has tipped towards the publicists' (Gamson, 1994, p.90). However, a factor that we need to bear in mind in analysing this story is that it may well have been distorted to make for an effective anecdote, by the editor who refused to be co-opted by Candice Bergen's team of people.

What kinds of persona (see Chapter 1) were the celebrities and their publicists working to achieve? In the first quotation, the big star was trying to move his image upmarket, away from tabloid television and towards more serious publications. The aim of the publicist in the second quotation was to present the star as a serious actor – an aim that, for some reason, perhaps through boredom or rebellion against the publicity tasks he was being asked to carry out, he chose to undermine. In the third, the aim was to bring out Candice Bergen's wit – perhaps because she wanted to build on TV success by taking on further comedy roles.

Such quotations cannot be taken as providing factual evidence of what happens in media organisations. However, they help us to think about the intentions and strategies of different groups of media workers, and how they work with, and against, each other. There is an important further purpose to investigating the practices and the thoughts of media workers. Such studies suggest that media products such as newspaper and magazine articles or television programmes take the form they do not because of the coming together of a random set of events on the one hand (which is how media workers often say that they see their work) or the intrinsic qualities of what is being reported on the other (say, because the particular celebrity is especially talented, or witty), but because of conventionalised ways in which media professionals go about things. Once again, what this gets across is something common to a great deal of empirical work in sociology: that social processes that might seem almost natural are actually very much constructed artefacts. Fame is *produced*. Organisational studies also hint at the importance of examining the interests of particular groups of people involved in such constructions. These interests will often coincide, but they will often clash too. Gamson shows how an examination of the working practices of media professionals can throw light both on the processes by which the media come to us and on the forms that media products take.

3 A political economy approach: celebrity as a means of controlling risk

The sociology of media organisations, then, can certainly be informative about how the media manufactures celebrity. However, some would argue that organisational approaches such as that illustrated by Gamson's research are in fact more limited than may meet the eye; that they are certainly not adequate in themselves for an understanding of the role of the media in contemporary societies (which some would see as the ultimate aim of media studies); and that they would therefore be inadequate for understanding the phenomenon of celebrity. Here, for example, is one writer, Edward Herman, talking about organisational studies of the production of news:

> [T]hey focus too heavily on organizational criteria of choice, often illustrated by struggles within the media as told by media personnel. They suffer from a lack of theory and measurement of actual media output. As a result, they tend to exaggerate the potential media professionals have for dissent and 'space', and to neglect how the usual news choices reinforce the status quo.
>
> Herman, 1995, p.81

Even though Herman is talking about organisational sociologies of journalism, his criticisms are a useful starting point for developing criticisms of organisational approaches more generally. He initially points to the problem, already signalled earlier, that the organisational approach might be too reliant on the way in which media professionals see their world. The implication here is that media professionals might be too involved in their world to have much perspective on it, that there will be aspects or implications of their work of which they are unaware. Herman also suggests that organisational studies might be under-theorised, that they might be too concerned with the description of particular events and not interested enough in the systematic explanation of practices. He criticises organisational studies for not measuring output (Herman favours a form of textual analysis – see Chapter 2 – known as content analysis, which counts items in particular media texts in an attempt to achieve an objective appraisal of media trends). Finally, Herman claims that organisational studies can miss the ways in which the media support existing hierarchies and inequalities in society.

This last point is especially significant here. Herman takes a critical political economy approach to the media. Critical political economy approaches aim to understand the economy in relation to political, social and cultural life, rather than seeing the economy as a fully separate domain. They engage not so much with questions of economic efficiency, which tend to be the main concerns of orthodox economists, but more with ethical questions of justice, equity and the public good (see Golding and Murdock, 2000). Critical political economy approaches to the media (called 'political economy approaches' from here on) strive to analyse the media in terms of their relations with the economic, political and cultural dimensions of society. They take a radical left-wing, and sometimes explicitly Marxian, political position with regard to the media. I focus on this kind of political economy here, rather than conservative or liberal economic accounts, because political economy of the media has been so important in the analysis of media production (see **Downey, 2006** for a discussion of more liberal and conservative economic approaches). The crucial point here is that in taking this radical left-wing perspective, political economy approaches are different from organisational sociology approaches, which are often underpinned by a liberal–pluralist political perspective. Liberal–pluralist perspectives on societies emphasise the co-existence of competing groups and interests, with none dominating all of the time, whereas radical leftist perspectives stress continuing, systemic domination based on class, gender and ethnicity (see Gurevitch et al., 1982, pp.1–3).

A number of key themes have become associated with the political economy approach since its inception among radical sociologists in the 1960s:

- The ownership and control of the media by the wealthy and powerful.
- The increasing size and scope of transnational media corporations.
- The growing reach of the private sector and the shrinking of areas of public ownership.
- The effects of the above on media content and in particular the dissemination of content that reinforces social inequality.

How would political economy approaches explain and evaluate the phenomenon of celebrity? On the whole, they would tend either to condemn or ignore it. As we saw in Chapter 1, there has been a long history of condemning modern variants of celebrity. Two important forerunners of a political economy of the media, the German philosophers Theodor Adorno and Max Horkheimer, criticised celebrity culture as part of a polemic against 'the culture industry', their metaphorical term for the way in which cultural production under capitalism had become as much an industry of mass production as had the manufacturing industries of the mid-twentieth century (see Adorno and Horkheimer, 1979/1944).

Many political economy writers now consider that Adorno and Horkheimer's essay on the culture industry was overly polemical, and that it failed to analyse the complex and contradictory forms that media production could take (for example, Miège, 1989). Nevertheless, Adorno and Horkheimer's sense that the media industries on the whole produce standardised or debased products – including celebrity culture – is echoed in the attitudes of some key political economy writers. This has been manifested not so much in outright condemnations of contemporary culture, as in a reluctance to analyse anything considered trivial. As a consequence, there have been very few sustained analyses of celebrity from the approach of political economy (though see Drake, 2002).

However, there is nothing intrinsic to political economy approaches that should outlaw the analysis of celebrity. In order to assess the potential contribution of political economy to the study of media production and celebrity, we shall examine a particular type of political economy approach called 'the cultural industries approach' (see also Hesmondhalgh, 2002) and show how it might be applied to celebrity.

'Cultural industries' is the term used for those industries that produce goods the main purpose of which is aesthetic and informational, rather than utilitarian. The term very much overlaps with 'the media industries'. The cultural industries approach analyses media production by examining the distinctive features of the cultural industries as opposed to other industries, such as cars, steel, construction and pharmaceuticals. As we shall see, the relevance of this approach to the study of celebrity is that it shows how celebrity operates as a means – one means among a number of strategies – for dealing with the *uncertainty* that particularly plagues the producers of media and cultural goods.

Activity 3.1

Spend a minute or two noting down what you think is meant by 'risk'. Why do you think celebrity might be a useful tool for media industries in combating risk? ■ ■ ■

3.1 The cultural industries approach

We can first ask in what way media production is risky or uncertain. There are many factors (see Garnham, 1990, p.161 for an important account) but this is how one writer, David F. Prindle, puts the problem in *Risky Business*, his book about Hollywood film and television in the 1990s. The problems he outlines also apply to magazines, newspapers, CD albums and other media products, however.

> Although it is fairly easy to gauge the market for an art (say, movies) in general, it is nearly impossible to do so for a particular artistic product. Everyone knows that people love to see good movies; nobody knows which movies will be considered good by enough people to make them profitable. Many of the industry's huge box

office hits were originally turned down by various studios that thought they would be sure-fire failures: *Star Wars, Back to the Future*, and *Dances With Wolves*, to name only three. Conversely, since no one will produce a film expected to fail, it can be presumed that the studios that released *Pennies from Heaven, Howard the Duck*, and *Ishtar* thought that these movies would make money. Instead, they lost a total of $83 million in domestic rentals.

Prindle, 1993, pp.4–5

The cultural industries approach, then, emphasises the distinctive conditions of the media industries, including the distinctive forms of high risk: other industries also have high levels of risk, but risk in the media industries is not only high-level, it is *all-pervasive*. As Prindle puts it, people in media industries such as Hollywood film and television, 'face the incalculable every day. Each choice is a stab in the dark, every decision a wager against unknown odds' (1993, p.5).

So the cultural industries approach emphasises the importance of the strategies adopted by media businesses for dealing with uncertainty. These are collectively distinct from the strategies used by other industries to deal with their own versions of uncertainty. And celebrity has an important function in a number of these strategies. The most important for our purposes here are as follows:

- *Throwing mud against the wall: over-production.* Because it is so difficult to predict what will be a hit, media businesses compensate by releasing a great deal of product onto markets. If only one in ten records is a hit, then releasing 50 clearly makes more sense than releasing five. This suggests that there is intense competition over who will emerge as celebrities within the various fields of media production. It also suggests that large companies will be better placed to deal with uncertainty through over-production than small companies.

- *Letting people know: the importance of circulation.* Media products have not only to be produced, they also have to be *circulated* – this means the distribution, marketing and publicising of media products. Whereas the organisational sociology approach makes clear the importance of marketing and publicity behind celebrities, and how celebrities are used to promote media products, the cultural industries approach offers an *explanation* of this importance. The cultural industries approach links the importance of marketing and publicity to the need to counter risk in the interests of making profit and shows how this helps lead to the growth of large private media corporations with considerable power and influence.

- *The big get bigger: integration.* Like many other industries, the media industries are characterised by strategies that deal with risk by attempting to dominate or expand markets. The most basic form of integration is horizontal: companies buy up competitors. Because of the importance of circulation, vertical integration is also vital. A company can be said to be vertically integrated when it is involved in different stages of the production process. So if a film production company buys a chain of cinemas in which to show its films, this involves vertical integration. Here the cultural industries approach offers a systematic explanation of the constant tendency towards certain forms of integration, and this helps to explain why celebrities increasingly circulate across different media. It makes sense for a corporation to put their recording artists into films they distribute, and on to TV channels they control. Again, there is also strong emphasis here on the problems that occur when large media companies come to dominate media markets and when they gain a substantial role in how societies communicate with each other (see **Downey, 2006**).

■ *The same but different: formatting.* An Australian cultural industries analyst, Bill Ryan, has provided a detailed analysis of the two main ways in which media businesses have come to rationalise the potentially chaotic nature of making cultural or media products. The media industries 'format' the production of their goods, Ryan explains, differentiating between products created primarily as *name-based* goods, associated with particular star actors, authors, musicians and so on; and those that are more *type-based* (Ryan, 1992). For example, book publishing companies produce literary novels and historical works that are organised around the individual style and/or vision of the author. However, they also produce books in which the author's individual vision is much less important, and in which the production process aims to offer a set of pleasures based around a particular genre, such as the romance. Such formatting is very important in the marketing of the product, as we shall see, not only because it helps companies fit marketing to production, but also because it gives audiences an indication of what kinds of pleasures are on offer. The formatted production of media texts according to genre or star usually finds its echoes in marketing: genre products will be marketed generically, name-based products will be marketed by star (see Chapter 2).

All this suggests a very important way in which celebrity matters in media production. Celebrity, via the creation and maintenance of stars, serves as a way of formatting and marketing media products, and therefore of reducing, or at least controlling, the uncertainty that the cultural industries approach sees as endemic in media production. We can explore this point in a little more detail by analysing how media companies market their products by each of the main formats referred to above: stars and genres.

Activity 3.2

Look at the CD covers in Plates 2 to 7 (in the colour section) and try to answer the following questions.

- What are the main differences between the CD covers marked (a) in the caption and those marked (b) in the caption?

- Try to make notes about what the images on each album sleeve suggest about the music contained within it. What does each suggest about the experiences on offer? ■ ■ ■

You may have been struck by the prominence on the sleeves marked (b) of the name of the artist; whereas on the sleeves marked (a) greater visual emphasis is placed on the title of the album. In each case, the (a) titles give a strong sense of the type of music contained on the albums to their potential buyers. In one case, *Classic Soul Volume 1*, the genre is explicit in the title, and then further information is given on the sleeve. *Son of Redneck* and *Classic Soul Volume 1* imply their genres (new or alternative country and soul, respectively), and give further information in their sub-titles. The sleeves marked (b) are clearly based on formatting according to the *name of the artist*, whereas those labelled (a) are being produced and marketed according to *genre*.

Each of the CD covers says a great deal about the music contained on the album. The cover of *Classic Soul Volume 1* features a singer, with his head thrown back, as if he is lost in the emotion of his performance. Soul is a musical genre that places great emphasis on the expressive and sensitive performance of vocalists. Even the presence of the singer's fingers, gently cradling the microphone, suggests a human touch, a certain sensitivity. The muted shades of the album's colouring recall those of classic jazz albums of the 1960s, suggesting that this is not just any soul compilation, but one of 'quality', appealing to a more discriminating audience. (This is confirmed by the back cover of the CD sleeve, which claims that the compilation series, *Mastercuts*, will 'endeavor [*sic*] to provide a higher standard of track listings, quality music and packaging' than other compilations.) *Son of Redneck*'s cover image suggests the wide open spaces associated with country music, and the incongruous presence of a Cadillac in a field suggests not only mobility through such spaces – this is driving music, perhaps? – but also that a new take on country clichés might be on offer.

The three star-artist albums all give prominence to their artists' names, but they have very different ways of presenting messages about those artists, all of which say different things about the use of star-artists to promote music. The Bob Marley and the Wailers sleeve features the

1970s' Jamaican reggae star Marley smoking a huge spliff. There is rebellion here, but also a strong sense of Marley as exotic to potential white buyers. He is shirtless in what may well be a Jamaican sun. There is thoughtfulness too in his frown. His eyes are shaded, suggesting depth. A possible pun in the title becomes apparent: lighting the spliff, but also social conflagration, a theme of many of the songs on the album. So the cover tells us that Marley embodies a particular form of thoughtful subversion.

The Blur album shows a very different way in which packaging might make a statement about an artist. The band themselves are not even pictured on the front, and many rock acts have used this to suggest a lack of interest in publicity (and this implies a greater interest in creativity). Instead, we have a fiercely aggressive image of two greyhounds racing. Greyhound racing is a distinctively British working-class pastime – the band are pictured at a greyhound track on the back cover – and the album in fact features a number of songs about contemporary British working-class life. The cover suggests a dark side to Blur's picture of this world, but also perhaps something funny and acerbic in their portrayal. The way that the photograph picks out the intensity of the dogs perhaps implies that Blur are shrewd observers of the strangeness of the everyday.

Plate 5 shows another artist image. I have selected this image to show that some artists are promoted and packaged in a way that suggests not only their distinctive appearance and personality, but also, before they become established as stars, that they might be associated with a particular genre. Here Nas is featured prominently, but his cool, direct stare, his clothing and styling and the urban landscape behind him all combine to give a strong indication of the genre within which he works: hip hop.

Not all of these meanings would be apparent to a casual browser in a record shop, and you may not agree with all my interpretations (see Chapter 2). However, you might agree that the covers suggest that stars and genres represent very different ways in which media companies market their products and that this marketing represents, in the case of stars, an attempt to attach certain meanings to the creators of media products. Ideally, a series of albums can then be marketed, using the particular star persona, or image, as an enticement to audiences. (Persona or image is meant in the broadest sense, referring not only to appearance but also to how a person's beliefs, attitudes and musical sounds are marked out as distinctive by marketers, and understood by the audience as such; see the discussion in Chapter 1.)

Activity 3.3

Based on what you have read so far, make some notes on what you think
the cultural industries approach, as a branch of political economy, offers the
study of celebrity. ▪ ▪ ▪

Much more than organisational approaches, political economy approaches
attempt to explain and evaluate recurring features of the media industries
and of their products. The cultural industries approach, for example,
seeks to explain why circulation (the distribution and marketing of goods)
is so central to power in the media industries, and it looks at the
consequences of this central role. While organisational approaches operate
at the micro level, as we saw in Section 2, examining particular moments
and processes in some detail, political economy approaches work at more
of a macro, or large-scale, level. The cultural industries approach is a type
of political economy approach that allows for some movement between
the macro and the micro, because it tries to show how the goal of
producing a profit has implications in the strategies adopted by
organisations. Its main orientation, like that of political economy
approaches more generally, is to contribute to debates about the degree
to which the profit imperative damages those societies, cultures and
economies that centre their production upon it, for example by creating
private corporations with enormous resources. These private corporations
do not always act in the public interest and there are many debates about
the degree to which their domination of media markets and of public
communication affect the kind of media culture we have.

Although there is no space to pursue this fully here, a political
economy/cultural industries approach might explain and evaluate the
increasing emphasis on celebrity in contemporary media culture via a
number of interrelated factors. As we saw in Activity 3.2, media products
are distinguished from each other partly on the basis of the names of the
people associated with them. Some of these names become stars, which
enables greater powers of recognition. As leisure time and disposable
income have grown in the advanced industrial countries, media
consumption and production have expanded. Stars and celebrities have
become more and more important as a way of distinguishing a mass of
products from each other. For a relatively small number of A-list star
celebrities in a variety of fields, from sport to film to art, this has led to
massive financial reward. Meanwhile, there is a proliferation of minor
celebrities (William Snape is just one example) as newspapers, magazines
and dozens of television stations try to attract attention to their products.
In terms of evaluation, a political economy account might well want to
be critical of a system where certain individuals are rewarded so hugely,
while thousands of other performers and creators, many of them
arguably just as talented as the A-listers, and arguably more talented than

the minor celebrities produced by television soaps and reality-TV shows, can barely make a living (see Drake, 2002 for one such account; see also the discussion in Chapter 1). It might also point to the way in which the vast payments required by A-list stars further enhance the power of the large private corporations that dominate media production, because only these corporations can afford them.

Political economists would therefore argue that their approach is better equipped to explain and evaluate media production and celebrity than the organisational approach. However, those sociologists drawn more to the study of everyday life in media organisations might respond that their close studies allow for a more grounded appreciation of what actually happens in those organisations. There are those who would accuse some versions of political economy of treating organisations as if they were merely transmitters of ideas that favour the powerful. Life in media organisations, they might say, is more complex, messy and interesting than that – and Gamson's work demonstrates this.

We have examined a number of differences between the organisational sociology approach of Gamson, and the cultural industries approach to celebrity presented here. But there are points of similarity too. Like the organisational approach discussed earlier, the cultural industries approach provides insight into why media products take the form they do. As presented here, though, it could be argued that the two approaches also share some significant problems and weaknesses. For example, we have said little so far about history (see Chapter 1). There is no reason why organisational approaches should not be imbued with history, and indeed many are, but the tendency is to concentrate on contemporary case studies, in part because of the difficulties of getting access to personal accounts and documents about organisational life from years ago. Some political economy approaches are very historical in orientation, but many studies focus mainly on recent changes in the media. I turn next to an approach that would claim to put historical issues much more firmly in the centre of the analytical picture. More importantly for our immediate purposes, it is also an approach that offers a very different notion of *power* from that at work in the two approaches we have examined so far.

4 A post-structuralist approach: celebrity as a system of discourses

A study by a Canadian academic, David Marshall, provides the opportunity to examine an approach to celebrity that is very much influenced by post-structuralism. His book, *Celebrity and Power* (1997), also has a considerable amount to say about media production and institutions and their relationship to celebrity and society. For Marshall, inspired in part by the work of the French historian Michel Foucault, celebrity is a set of discourses that regulate the relationships between what it means to be an individual and what it means to be part of a wider collective identity. Even though Foucault has exercised an enormous influence on social and cultural theory in the decades since his death in 1984, his work has been taken up surprisingly rarely in media studies. However, for the purposes of this chapter, his work offers a third way into understanding media production, because Foucault and his many admirers would tend to be critical both of organisational sociology approaches and of political economy approaches.

4.1 A Foucauldian approach to power and celebrity

The most obvious way in which Marshall is indebted to Foucault is in his focus on, and understanding of, *power*. Marshall sees celebrity as involving a different and less definable form of power than those forms invested in institutions such as legislative assemblies, government bureaucracies and even the media themselves. He draws on a wide variety of theories to study celebrity, but his main source is Foucault. Marshall (1997, p.71) contrasts Foucault's approach to power favourably with those approaches that would see power 'in terms of opposition between those who possess power and those who do not'. This may at first sight seem absurd: isn't power all about whether you've got it or not? Not according to Foucault. He draws attention to the *dispersed* ways in which power operates and to how power can be *internalised*. Foucault's method was often to show how modern forms of power have developed in ways that are distinct from previous, more directly repressive forms of power. This means that, rather than seeing power as vested primarily in the state, or in businesses and producers (as political economy approaches would), we might instead see power as much more dispersed and widespread, and yet operating on a smaller scale in institutions such as the family, schools, medicine and so on. This has important political implications. Both liberal–pluralists and socialists would see the state as a key locus for political action. Marxists would emphasise the importance of the ownership of the means of production. Foucault's approach suggests that political action is possible and desirable in a whole host of places neglected by radical left and liberal–pluralist theory. It is easy to see why Foucault has been very fashionable in an era of new social movements based around questions of identity and experience, such as feminism, queer activism, environmentalism and so on. Marshall picks up this approach by examining the politics of entertainment.

Central to much of Foucault's work was the idea that power works primarily through *discourses*, or through discursive formations, sets of social rules and knowledges that govern what it is possible to say, do and know on any topic (see, for example, Foucault, 1979; see the discussion of discourse in Chapter 1, Section 3). For Marshall, celebrity provides social rules and knowledges that regulate the relationships between being an individual and being part of a wider collective identity. To explain this, Marshall points to two contradictory representations of personal and collective power in modern western democracies. One is that all individuals have power, whether as citizens or consumers; the other is that democracy means that the collective will is all-powerful. But there has been considerable anxiety about the collective will in modern life. Large collectivities have become associated for many with the non-rational and the emotional. Think of the connotations of words such as 'the mass', 'the mob' or 'the crowd'. Collectivities are often seen as volatile and dangerous in much modern thought, but they are desirable too. If the masses can be controlled and contained, they can act as consumers for products or as voters who can legitimate the authority of rulers.

In Marshall's view, celebrity helps to do this. This links to a further reason why Marshall thinks celebrity is important. Modern life involves complex relationships between, on the one hand, efforts to run systems on the basis of reason, to rationalise social processes and, on the other, the way in which human beings continue to be driven by non-rational aspects of themselves. Celebrity provides the opportunity to think about how the non-rational domain of the emotions (the *affective* domain, as it is sometimes called) has important social implications. (This emphasis on emotions and affect is Marshall's own contribution to the debate, not a feature of Foucault's work.)

4.2 The role of the entertainment industries

This is where media production comes in. According to Marshall, the entertainment industries construct celebrities and these celebrities play two very significant roles in modern life in mass, democratic societies. The first role is that celebrities act as representative embodiments for the rest of us of what it is like to be an individual (see Book Introduction and Chapter 2). The idea here seems to be that we witness the struggles of celebrities over how they present themselves to the world and relate this to our own efforts to present ourselves. As Marshall (1997, p.246) puts it, 'the celebrity is the independent individual par excellence'. The discourses of celebrity today suggest the possibility that anyone can achieve successful individuality by sheer force of will (see the discussion of the populist perspective on celebrity in Chapter 1). The second function of celebrities in Marshall's account is that they serve to control the masses, and to channel their emotional energies. The entertainment industries produce a variety of celebrities who can act as brand names, organising mass taste into marketable units for consumption (in this respect, Marshall echoes the cultural industries approach) and who can also act as points of identification for audiences in a society in which other forms of collective identity, such as class and ethnicity, are arguably becoming looser. In other words, celebrities provide key ways in which people come together but, according to Marshall, in containable ways, rather than as groups that might be more disruptive of social order.

Particular entertainment industries tend to suggest particular forms of affective identification with celebrities for their audiences. Marshall provides a comparison of film and television (and in this he strongly echoes Langer, 1981 – see Chapter 2, Section 3.1). Let us take the example of the film industry first. Through an analysis of the career of Tom Cruise, Marshall argues that film celebrities tend to develop in a way that draws on, but also reinforces, film's high prestige within media culture. Film actors begin by representing physical types and then develop a screen personality closely linked to a particular set of roles. But to achieve lasting celebrity, they must then 'transgress' the limitations of this initial screen personality by taking on roles at odds with it, and/or they must reveal a private self that is different from their screen personality (see Chapter 1, Section 3).

Cruise made his star name in films such as *Risky Business* (USA, dir. Brickman, 1983) and *Top Gun* (USA, dir. Scott, 1986) by creating a celebrity persona based on a youthful self-confidence (see Figure 3.4), but without the rebellion associated with earlier young stars such as James Dean and Paul Newman. Marshall argues that Cruise then had to transgress this persona in order to avoid repeating himself. Cruise took on roles such as the disabled Vietnam war veteran in *Born on the Fourth of July* (USA, dir. Stone, 1989) (see Figure 3.5) and the brother of an autistic man in *Rain*

Figure 3.4 Tom Cruise in Top Gun: *conformist self-confidence*

Figure 3.5 Tom Cruise in Born on the Fourth of July: *a bid for legitimation?*

Man (USA, dir. Levinson, 1988). Such roles involved teaming him up with 'serious', legitimated actors such as Dustin Hoffman and controversial directors such as Oliver Stone. In his private life (which is, of course, made public in publicity) his passionate relationship with Nicole Kidman and his interest in political causes added 'depth' to his persona. For Marshall, it is important that all this very consciously strategic work was aimed at making Cruise not only economically powerful, but also culturally legitimate. But it is also very important that film celebrities have to carry out so much work in order to maintain distance from their audience, to remain somehow out of their reach (see Chapter 2, Section 3.1). They do this by moving on when there is a danger that they will become too familiar. Film celebrity works by creating an aura that the audience admires from afar. Now let us turn to Marshall's discussion of television.

Reading 3.4 Activity

Now read the following extract from David Marshall , *Celebrity and Power* (Reading 3.4) and then make notes on the following questions:

- According to Marshall, what are the main characteristics of typical television celebrities?
- How does this relate to the distinctive characteristics of television as a medium?
- What contrasts does he draw with film celebrities?

Reading 3.4

David Marshall, 'The television celebrity: identification with the familiar'

With the television celebrity we are drawn to think of the talk-show personality or the news anchor as standing in for us or representing our interests. The celebrity's interests are painted as if they originate from an audience. In the talk-show format, a style of television production that dominates the televisual universe, the host constructs familiarity with the studio audience setting and the continuous touring of the audience for questions and comments for the assembled guests. In the case of Oprah, this familiarity leads to a sympathetic form of identification and is buttressed by occasional program episodes that have personal relevance to her life. Occasionally, episodes of her show have focused on themes directly related to her 'private battles' concerning her history as an abused child or, alternatively, her battle with diets and weight loss. Oprah as hero is presented as vulnerable and subject to weaknesses that others suffer.

Audiences are thus constructed to be loyal and therefore regular viewers of her program; they are drawn to her candor, which allows her to move seamlessly from the public sphere to the private in her presentation of self. There is a virtual public acknowledgement that her audience is aware of her 'private battles'; her private life, in general, is not constructed as a separate and private realm and is unified with her public performances. Her power as a sympathetic hero is dependent on her presenting herself as both honest and open.

The specific case of Oprah reveals some general features about the construction of the television celebrity that relate to television's difference as a medium. The familial feel of television and its celebrities is also a play with verisimilitude. The construction of a news reality and the various forms of live and simulated live television that dominate the television schedule are all aspects of television's efforts to represent a truer-to-life form of cultural expression. Whereas film has moved to the fictional and sometimes an aesthetic construction of its meanings, television concentrates on representing the real. Even in much of its special dramatic programming, an often favored formula is the docudrama, where a specific and topical issue is tackled in a fictionalized way. [...] The television image can be seen as less embellished and less crafted and therefore closer to the real and the everyday [than the filmic image]. One can see television's different play with the real through the soap opera's generally poor production values and the continuity of story lines so that they resemble everyday life. In situation comedy, the general familial feel of the stories and casts also makes them closer to the everyday. Both sitcoms and soap operas are constructed to fit into the rituals of everyday life through the regularity of their presentation. [...]

The implication for the television celebrity is that he or she is structured to reinforce the feeling of close proximity to the real and the familial. The TV celebrity is more accessible than the film celebrity. He or she is seen on a more regular basis, in the serial format of television programs. The auratic distance is less central to the television celebrity. The pretensions of an aesthetic abstraction are also underplayed. The codes of acting are replaced by the similitude of the television character with the television star's supposed real life; the break that defines the independence and autonomy of the film star is less significant in the construction of the television celebrity.

Reading source

Marshall, 1997, pp.190–2 ■ ■ ■

For Marshall, television constructs a discourse of sympathetic familiarity around its stars (see Figure 3.6 and Plate 8 in the colour section of this book) that is in marked contrast to the 'auratic' distance between film celebrities and their audiences (an aura is a kind of glow emanating from a person; the idea here is that film celebrities are imbued with a kind of superhuman quality). This is closely related to features of the medium of television that, in Marshall's view, involve claims to realism, in contrast with the heightened fiction of cinema. Film celebrities draw on lofty aspirations to serious, legitimate culture, whereas television tends to aspire to the everyday. These two forms of celebrity represent different forms of individuality in contemporary culture, and different sets of potential identifications for audiences (see Chapter 4). Taken as a whole, though, for Marshall these celebrities, constructed through the entertainment industries, create the most powerful forms of identification in modern societies. They influence the construction of celebrity in other domains, including politics. But the crucial point for Marshall is that the production of such celebrities constitutes a (perpetually failing) attempt 'to control the mass' (p.243). The system of celebrity does this by focusing the attention of audiences on the private experiences of individuals as 'the ultimate site of truth and meaning for any representation in the public sphere' (p.247) (the Oxfam case in Chapter 1 is a good example of this). Ideas of concerted public action that may be socially disruptive and even dangerous are defused by focusing people's attention on the private realm.

Figure 3.6 Oprah with her TV audience: sympathetic familiarity

How convincing did you find all this? One of the great benefits of Marshall's piece is that he is greatly aware of the mediating effects of the different technologies through which we come to know celebrities (see Chapter 1). You might feel, however, that this all seems a little over-generalised. You might, for example, have thought of ways in which television carries great legitimacy and authority – for instance, when reporting on major crises such as war or the death of prominent public figures. There are high-prestige drama programmes and TV awards ceremonies along the lines of the Oscars. In addition, the film industry produces huge amounts of low-grade, unprestigious product. Film celebrities can go down the prestige ladder as well as up. Marshall is at pains to point out that television tends to *privilege* sympathetic identification, rather than being entirely reliant on it, but he does seem to be making very clear distinctions between the media of film and television. Those drawn to the organisational approach might claim that Marshall does not pay enough attention to the ways in which celebrity has been produced on an everyday level, that he does not ground his analysis enough in the everyday operations of media organisations, past and present.

There are other problems that adherents of liberal–pluralist and radical left political perspectives might want to point out. One problem with Foucault's account of power, according to some of his many critics (for example, Fraser, 1989), is that power becomes a catch-all concept, blurring very different notions such as force, authority, violence and legitimation. It also loses its connection with any clear sense of domination and inequality. Political economists on the radical left – and indeed many in the centre of the political spectrum – would say that the reason why power is of political interest is precisely because of its potential links with these other processes. In Marshall's account, celebrity seems to have tremendous 'power' to control the mass and yet there is no clear sense of the sources of such power. Who wants to control the masses and why? Marshall is silent on such issues – whereas political economists would perhaps want to attribute such developments to the domination of a particular class.

Another potential problem is that the entertainment industries seem enormously important in Marshall's account and yet Marshall provides no explanation of how the entertainment industries come to take their key role in modern societies. Political economists would wonder whether there is some sort of connection between the economic interests of the media industries and the interests of other powerful groups in society as they stake claims to political power.

Defenders of post-structuralism and more particularly of Marshall's approach might want to make a number of comments in response. They might argue that it is worth taking the risk of ambitious generalisation from detailed specific case studies, in order to paint a broader historical picture of celebrity, media and power in modern societies, and of how values and beliefs propagated by the media shape ideas throughout society. They might also point to the way in which Marshall tackles the non-rational and emotional dimensions of human beings full on and takes seriously their possible implications. As you may have noticed, we are a world away here from political economy approaches, which tend to see emotion and affect as interference in forms of communication, such as public affairs journalism, which ought in their view to be oriented towards free and reasoned exchange of information, ideas and viewpoints. As for the accusations that post-structuralist accounts neglect debates about causation, it might be argued in response that Marxian quests for an explanation of social processes make the understanding of particular institutions and practices subordinate to an account of the whole, based on grand schemes of class conflict. The post-structuralists would perhaps claim that they are involved in more realistic and pragmatic descriptions of how institutions create our ideas about the world.

5   Conclusion: applying the approaches to celebrities and to celebrity culture

At the beginning of this chapter we had two main aims: to examine how we might understand celebrity by looking at media production; and to introduce and explain three different approaches to media production and celebrity. Table 3.1 provides a summary of the approaches. As you will see, this includes a brief summary of what each approach tells us about celebrity. In this section, we shall review these comments further and apply them to two case studies.

First of all, let us review what we have learnt about celebrity and media production. There were significant divergences between the different approaches and this means that this question needs to be answered somewhat provisionally accompanied by the qualification 'it depends which perspective you're taking'. The first approach, the organisational sociology approach taken by Gamson, understood media production as the subjective world of producers. Focusing on the micro level, this approach was able, through interviews and the study of relevant texts, to show in some detail how celebrities are made and marketed on an everyday basis. There is an almost wide-eyed wonder at the sheer amount of co-ordinated, negotiated complex social work involved behind the scenes of celebrity. The second approach, the cultural industries approach, provides a more cool-headed appreciation of media production as a field constrained by perennial uncertainty. It attempts systematic explanation of how media producers respond to such

Table 3.1 The three approaches to media production and celebrity

Approach to media production and celebrity	Main example used in chapter	Main emphases of approach	Political perspective	Methods	What does the approach tell us about celebrity?	Limitations in analysing media
Organisational sociology approach	Gamson (1994)	Micro, not macro; empiricist?; focuses on actions and views of media workers	Liberal–pluralist	Interviews with media professionals; documents; participant observation	Celebrity is produced and constructed by concerted, co-operative action	Exaggerates freedom of media workers? Reliant on media workers' accounts? Too descriptive and not concerned enough with power?
Political economy approach ('the cultural industries approach')	Author's synthesis of various, including Ryan (1992)	Explanation and evaluation at macro level (ethical questions of equity and public good); distinctive conditions of media production for profit	Radical left, often Marxian	Systemic analysis of distinctive strategies of media businesses	Celebrity a means of boosting profit and controlling uncertainty; could evaluate celebrity in terms of reinforcement of inequalities of power and wealth	(Political economy approaches as a whole): Entertainment/celebrity seen as trivial. Too much on production, not enough on subjectivity and identity?
Poststructuralist approach	Marshall (1997)	Historical orientation; dispersed and internalised nature of power; emphasis on affect and emotion	Critical of liberal–pluralism and Marxism	Historical analysis, detailed examination of representation	Celebrity is a set of discourses about individuality and collectivity; and about rationalisation and emotion in public life	Power becomes a catch-all concept? Lack of explanation and clear evaluation? Role of media industries unclear at times

uncertainty in systemic ways. Celebrity can be seen as a strategy for the containment of commercial uncertainty, a way of linking products together, of branding them. Finally, Marshall's Foucauldian study transcends Gamson's very specific case study to take a wider view that sees media production as highly dependent on technologies of dissemination. Marshall makes a stimulating effort to delineate the way in which media producers create a range of potential emotional relationships for audiences. And he draws attention to the way in which celebrity has an important role in shaping how we think about personal and collective identity.

We have examined various examples throughout this chapter. However, to clarify the approaches further, we can look briefly at how they might address the same celebrity case studies. We will examine two very different examples in order to test the approaches across the spectrum from politics to entertainment (many political leaders in the media age are, after all, celebrities).

Activity 3.4

Before reading on, try to construct how each of the three approaches would examine the current President of the United States of America, or any past President, as a celebrity. What insights might each approach provide? What might be the potential problems in using each approach? Now try the same exercise for whoever you consider to be the world's most famous pop star. ■ ■ ■

We can take Bill Clinton and Michael Jackson as examples here. (The fact that these celebrities might now be less famous than they used to be can actually be an advantage in carrying out an analysis – it makes the analysis less likely to be overtaken by further developments than if the current President of the United States and this week's Number 1 recording artist were being discussed.) The organisational sociology approach would probably proceed by interviewing those workers primarily responsible for the construction of Clinton's and Jackson's personae at various points during their careers. It might analyse books and other publications dealing with political PR in order to gain a sense of how these media workers understand their job and the particular nature of the challenge confronting them. The approach would examine how each of them achieved fame and how they sustained it. A major problem in both cases would be gaining access to the key people involved. Interviews with those still working as publicists with either celebrity would be compromised by anxieties about confidentiality. This is especially so, given that both these celebrities share, across the politics/ entertainment divide, the common challenge of having had to rescue their celebrity reputation from the taint of sexual scandal. Yet organisational sociology might be better at addressing how celebrities deal with such negative publicity than the other approaches. However, interviews regarding events further back in time (say, Jackson's rise to fame in the early 1970s as a child superstar, or Clinton's election as Governor of Arkansas) would be compromised by the problems of remembering that far back or of accessing documents from the time.

The cultural industries approach would analyse how both celebrities owe their fame to the shape and structure of the contemporary media. Clinton, for example, like any political leader, provides a focus of interest for news media that helps build or maintain audiences and fill space. Jackson was used as a star name to sell albums that consumers would buy, knowing that they were likely to hear a certain sound. The cultural industries approach would analyse how he came to occupy such a central position in the star system of the recording industry in the 1980s and early 1990s, and how his earning power translated into a great deal of wealth and of power vis-à-vis recording companies. Like other types of political economy approach, the cultural industries approach might well criticise the way in which celebrities such as Jackson help to expand the size and scope of already powerful media corporations. However, this approach would only tell us a limited amount about the political and cultural conditions surrounding the production of these celebrities.

A post-structuralist approach to these celebrities, along the lines developed by Marshall, would look at the historical development of understandings of political leadership and of musical stardom, especially as it relates to the particular period in which Clinton and Jackson achieved and sustained their fame. Such an approach might stress how Clinton drew upon forms of self-presentation developed in the entertainment industries and how he studied the way in which television performers established a rapport with their audiences. It might emphasise the way in which a new development in media, the rise of the music video on cable and satellite television channels, helped to crystallise Jackson's celebrity, creating a new type of intimacy between popular music stars and their audiences – an intimacy at a great distance, as it were. If the earlier criticisms made of Marshall's approach are accurate, however, these accounts may lack clarity in terms of how they explain and evaluate the phenomenon of celebrity.

In this chapter we have seen that the study of the media via production is an important and interesting way to find out about any media-related phenomenon such as celebrity. But as this brief application of the approaches to two globally famous Americans makes clear, and as we emphasise throughout this book, the study of any one aspect of the production–texts–audiences trio is never enough to understand any media-related phenomenon. All aspects need to be understood in relation to the other dimensions, so any adequate analysis of Jackson and Clinton would also need to take account of their meanings at particular moments, and of the way in which different audiences and publics understand them. This was apparent at various points in the chapter, where techniques of textual analysis were brought to bear on publicity texts, vital to the production and circulation of goods. It was also apparent where Marshall discussed the way in which the entertainment industries produce certain kinds of 'subject position' for their audiences (a topic which is discussed further in the next chapter).

All the approaches offer important insights into the phenomenon of celebrity. They all help us to see that fame is socially produced, through the concerted and organised efforts of groups of media personnel, rather than something which happens randomly, or as a result of individual talent. However, the approaches cannot simply be added one to the other to create the best possible account. There are real political and methodological tensions underlying the differences between these approaches and in many respects, though not all, they are incommensurable. This means that choices about which approach to take to the media, to media production and to celebrity, are by no means innocent or arbitrary ones. As we have seen, such decisions involve important, difficult and controversial questions about what we want to know, how to go about investigating it and, perhaps most crucially, how we think research on media ought to contribute to larger debates about the nature of society.

Further reading

Gamson, J. (1994) *Claims to Fame*, Berkeley, CA, University of California Press.

Golding, P. and Murdock, G. (2000) 'Culture, communications and political economy' in Curran, J. and Gurevitch, M. (eds) *Mass Media and Society* (3rd edn), London, Arnold.

Hesmondhalgh, D. (2002) *The Cultural Industries*, London, Sage.

Marshall, P.D. (1997) *Celebrity and Power: Fame in Contemporary Culture*, Minneapolis, MN, University of Minnesota Press.

Negus, K. (1997) 'The production of culture' in du Gay, P. (ed.) *Production of Culture/Cultures of Production*, London, Sage/The Open University.

References

Adorno, T.W. and Horkheimer, M. (1979/1947) 'The culture industry: enlightenment as mass deception' in Curran, J. and Gurevitch, M. (eds) *Mass Communications and Society*, London, Edward Arnold.

Downey, J. (2006) 'The media industries: do ownership, size and internationalisation matter?' in Hesmondhalgh, D. (ed.) *Media Production*, Maidenhead, Open University Press/The Open University (Book 3 in this series).

Drake, P. (2002) *Stardom After the Star System: Economies of Performance in Contemporary Hollywood Cinema*, PhD thesis, University of Glasgow.

Foucault, M. (1979) *The History of Sexuality, Vol.1: An Introduction* (trans. R. Hurley), London, Allen Lane.

Fraser, N. (1989) *Unruly Practices: Power, Discourse and Gender in Contemporary Social Theory*, Minneapolis, MN, University of Minnesota Press.

Gamson, J. (1994) *Claims to Fame*, Berkeley, CA, University of California Press.

Garnham, N. (1990) *Capitalism and Communication*, London, Sage.

Golding, P. and Murdock, G. (2000) 'Culture, communications and political economy' in Curran, J. and Gurevitch, M. (eds) *Mass Media and Society* (3rd edn), London, Edward Arnold.

Gurevitch, M., Bennett, T., Curran, J. and Woollacott, J. (1982), *Culture, Society and the Media*, London, Methuen.

Herman, E. (1995) 'Media in the US political economy' in Downing, J., Mohammadi, A. and Sreberny-Mohammadi, A. (eds) *Questioning the Media: A Critical Introduction* (2nd edn), London, Sage.

Hesmondhalgh, D. (2002) *The Cultural Industries*, London, Sage.

Hesmondhalgh, D. (2006) 'The media's view of the audience' in Hesmondhalgh, D. (ed.) *Media Production*, Maidenhead, Open University Press/The Open University (Book 3 in this series).

Langer, J. (1981) 'Television's personality system', *Media, Culture and Society*, vol.4, pp.351–65.

Marshall, P.D. (1997) *Celebrity and Power: Fame in Contemporary Culture*, Minneapolis, MN, University of Minnesota Press.

Miège, B. (1989) *The Capitalization of Cultural Production*, New York, International General.

Negus, K. (1997) 'The production of culture' in du Gay, P. (ed.) *Production of Culture/Cultures of Production*, London, Sage/The Open University.

Prindle, D. (1993) *Risky Business*, Boulder, CO, Westview Press.

Rein, I., Kotler, P and Stoller, M. (1997) *High Visibility: The Making and Marketing of Professionals into Celebrities*, Chicago, IL, NTC Business Books.

Ryan, B. (1992) *Making Capital from Culture*, Berlin and New York, Walter de Gruyter.

Chapter 4

Audiences and celebrity

Nick Stevenson

Contents

1 Four approaches to audiences and celebrity

> TV channels now run weekly programmes in which popular records are played to teenagers and judged. While the music is performed, the cameras linger savagely over the faces of the audience. What a bottomless chasm of vacuity they reveal! ... Leaving a TV studio recently, I stumbled into the exodus from one of these sessions. How pathetic and listless they seemed: young girls, hardly any more than 16, dressed as adults and already lined up as fodder for exploitation. Their eyes came to life only when one of their grotesque idols – scarcely older than they – made a brief appearance, before a man in a camel-hair coat hustled him into a car.
>
> Johnson, 1964, p.17

Taken from an article in the *New Statesman,* a left-wing British weekly, this quotation from Paul Johnson about 'the menace of Beatlism' reveals some profound anxieties about the nature of media audiences and, in particular, the audiences for celebrities (see Figure 4.1). The contempt and fear expressed here are not untypical and still persist in public life about the attachments that people – especially teenagers, and particularly girls – form with idols, icons and celebrities. You can perhaps see from your study of Chapters 1 and 3 how Johnson represents a 'cultural decline' position similar to certain members of the Frankfurt School – although it is theoretically far more simplistic. Theodor Adorno and Max Horkheimer (1979) argued that the media industries on the whole produce formulaic and standardised content that channels a passive and obedient response from audiences. But is it possible to go beyond the assumption that how audiences react is determined in advance by producers, to enable us to gain a more informed and thoughtful understanding of the way in which audiences relate to the media and to mediated celebrities in particular?

This chapter looks at four different ways in which writers on the media have attempted to understand the relationships between media texts, media audiences and celebrities. First, in the next section, we look at an approach which seeks to go beyond early twentieth-century fears about the charisma of individuals, to try and understand the popularity and charisma of mediated celebrities on the basis of how they 'resonate' with certain features of society. This involves a 'textual' reading of stars on the basis of which assumptions about audiences and their responses are made. This first approach is somewhat more sanguine about celebrity and audiences than that of theorists such as Johnson, quoted above. The second approach, which we explore in Section 3, is even more optimistic, because it sees identification with celebrities as a way of *resisting* some of

Figure 4.1 *Screaming fans at a Beatles concert, London, 1963*

the features that can be associated with living within unequal societies. Rather than a textual analysis of stars, this approach emphasises the importance of empirical methods such as interviews, where the researcher interacts with the audiences for media products (including audiences for celebrities). The third approach (Section 4) takes this 'optimistic', affirmative reading of audiences further by interpreting fans of celebrities and other media texts as 'ideal' audiences, in that they are particularly active (rather than the passive 'dopes' depicted by Johnson). The fourth approach (Section 5) is based on the suggestion that the study of media audiences and celebrity would do well to break with the basic assumptions connected with the simple opposition between optimistic and pessimistic interpretations of (celebrity) audiences, as negative or positive, as dominated or resistant.

The point of outlining these four approaches to celebrity and audiences is to show that the study of audiences can take a variety of forms in media analysis. The term 'approach' does not imply that these are fully worked-out theoretical perspectives; simply that they are different ways in which celebrity audiences can be understood. In this chapter, I want to map the different theoretical and methodological assumptions that inform these four approaches, and indicate the tensions that exist between them. I suggest that it is not necessary to choose one approach over others (although we may wish to do so), but we need to proceed carefully as some critical questions are better respected by certain intellectual traditions than others.

2 Charisma and beyond: why do celebrities 'resonate' with audiences?

2.1 The 'culture industry' thesis: fearing the charismatic individual

One way of understanding celebrities, as you saw in Chapter 1, Section 2, is that they are charismatic individuals. The German sociologist Max Weber argued that charisma represents a specific form of domination in the modern era. Weber described the charismatic individual as someone who is believed to possess superhuman qualities and capabilities. Weber was less concerned with whether specific individuals really had these qualities, and more with the fact that their followers attributed these to them. Charismatic leaders can be political or religious leaders who shape the development of civilisations or more everyday contexts. Charisma in this sense implies an irrational phenomenon that turns people into followers of leaders and icons.

Building on Weber's approach, the German philosopher Adorno (1991) argues that charismatic forms of domination are enhanced by the development of 'the culture industry' (see Chapters 1 and 2). He argues that the culture industry paved the way for the rise of authoritarian leaders across European societies during the 1930s and 1940s. In particular, Adorno focuses on the way in which fascist dictatorships were able to use the media of mass communication to promote their political interests. In Adorno's analysis of fascist propaganda he notes how extremist agitation is based upon the capacity of the masses to identify with a charismatic leader and he argues that the masses give up on their rational interests to identify with an all-powerful father-figure. Complex feelings are involved in this process. The people, Adorno reasons, are able to love their leader as a way of loving themselves. Hitler personified the idea of the 'great little man' who requires submission and the recognition that he is 'one of the people' (see Figure 4.2). These feelings of collective solidarity are further reinforced by projecting more ambivalent sentiments onto a hated out-group (the obvious case being people of Jewish descent).

Adorno is not suggesting that all charismatic individuals, such as celebrities, have the same power as Hitler, but he offers a warning as to how identification with powerful individuals can promote fascist and totalitarian ideologies.

Figure 4.2 Adolf Hitler at a Nazi rally in Nuremberg in 1927

Fascist propaganda, like the culture industry, seeks to move the individual between conformism and manufactured rebellion, inhibiting critical or independent forms of thinking. For example, in Adorno's view, the cliché-ridden speech of the fascist ultimately depends upon similar logics to be found elsewhere, such as in advertising and in the culture industry more generally.

Activity 4.1

Make notes on the following questions:

■ What do you think of Adorno's warning about the dangers of identification with powerful, charismatic individuals?

■ How do you think this can this be applied to modern celebrities? ■ ■ ■

There are some problems in applying Adorno's analysis to contemporary celebrity. It is perhaps pressing the point too far to link the adoration of celebrities with that required by totalitarian leaders. Yet there is clearly a connection between the forms of charisma required by a politician and those utilised by popular icons and celebrities. Indeed some would argue that politics itself has come to increasingly resemble a form of entertainment (see Chapter 1, Section 5). There is no room here to explore this further, but we can note that modern politics and the entertainment industries both require the production of representations of individuals who are instantly recognised by millions of people. Richard Dyer attempts to go beyond Adorno and Weber in a discussion of entertainment stars and charisma. He argues that theories of charisma are useful but problematic (Dyer, 1998). In so doing he endorses Francesco Alberoni's (1972) point that unlike a political leader, the status of a star does not depend upon having institutional or political power. However, as you have seen in Chapter 1, Section 4, there are perhaps increasing links between the two domains, for example, in the way in which pop stars and other celebrities have become involved in political campaigns (such as pop star Robbie Williams and UNICEF). For Dyer, the institutions involved in both politics and entertainment need to construct particular *images*, biographies and associations that makes a particular figure resonate with its time. So the issue for Dyer becomes: what is it about the persona of a particular star or politician that seems to resonate with so many people?

2.2 Resonance and historical context

This is an important question. It is not enough to assume that stars or celebrities resonate with audiences simply because they are made visible. There are plenty of examples in history of figures in popular film, music and television that either failed to catch on or who were once popular, but were then quickly forgotten. Think of the numerous television programmes and newspaper articles that ask of former celebrities 'where are they now?' In this respect, Dyer suggests, the charisma of stars and celebrities is different from that of political leaders in that they capture something of their time. For example, Dyer suggests that Marilyn Monroe was a star whose image captured a number of ideas of sexuality and morality in 1950s' USA. Monroe's charisma came from her ability to move between the twin poles of sexuality and innocence in such a way that characterised a society that was relaxing censorship laws, being challenged by the feminist movement and encountering the spread of affluence (see Figure 4.3).

We can also see similar ambiguities and tensions in other stars of the 1950s. The film star James Dean is often viewed as the iconic representation of post-war teenage rebellion. His image as 'the first teenager' comes from his performance as Jim Stark, a misunderstood adolescent in *Rebel Without a Cause* (USA, dir. Ray, 1955) (see Plate 12 in the colour plate section). This famous film suggests that being a teenager is a troubled period, indeed 'a time when nothing seems to fit'. The film's narrative, however, could easily be understood through a conservative lens where teenage confusion is the result of emasculated father-figures, absent parents and families that lack social discipline. Jim Stark's inner turmoil and confusion is largely shared by the other young people in the film who are all searching for something 'sincere' in a world where male authority and leadership has broken down. Seemingly it is the decline of social discipline and of paternal authority that have led to teenage unrest and confusion. Yet, it is doubtful that this is the message that has been taken from the film by successive generations of teenage viewers. Dean's troubled and uncertain masculinity coupled with his well-groomed image emphasises the liquid eyes, soft hair and lips that give him a feminine appearance. His ambiguous masculinity has been the basis of an enduring image of the moody and sensitive male. Dean offers an appearance of masculinity distinct from the clean-cut, patriotic, all-American boy that was the dominant norm of this period (Ehrenreich et al., 1991). So, while the media and popular culture of the 1950s may be seen in retrospect as compliant and conservative, it also made

Figure 4.3 *Marilyn Monroe, 1957*

visible new kinds of heterosexual masculinity. In *Rebel Without a Cause*, Dean is a subtle rebel, offering an image of uncertainty and ambiguity rather than conformity or outright rebellion. As Jim Stark in the movie, Dean neither rejects straight masculinity nor more angrily reaffirms it by adopting a tough-guy image. The important point, though, is that Dean and his image still have a considerable amount of resonance, and this probably says something about the relatively slow rate of change of masculine identities. Dean's continued charisma is sustained because his image continues to connect with the tensions of everyday life as experienced by teenagers.

Activity 4.2

Select two or three contemporary celebrities. These can be anyone (such as Tom Cruise, Eminem, Madonna or Julia Roberts). Why do you think these people resonate within our culture? What contemporary tensions or ambiguities do they seem to represent? How are they 'of our time'? ■ ■ ■

Dyer offers a way of reading celebrities in terms of charisma that may, in many respects, go beyond Adorno in offering a way of thinking about how *particular* entertainment stars – and even political leaders – 'resonate' with audiences. Madonna, for example, might 'resonate' because her performances and songs suggest a woman in control of experimenting with different sexual identities. This might connect with the idea of sexual freedom for women (which is not to say that women really are 'free').

However, you may have noticed that 'the audience' has been a distant feature in our discussion so far. The audience has only been *invoked* by the writers we have looked at, it has not yet appeared as an object of analysis in its own right. A number of academics working in media and cultural studies have tried to correct the bias implicit in previous forms of analysis. These studies have sought to insist upon a basic distinction between the social processes involved in production, in the meaning of texts, and in the moment of reception or consumption (see Book Introduction). The next section explores this issue.

3 Empirical studies of audiences

3.1 The fallacy of 'internalism'

For the British social theorist John B. Thompson (1990, p.105), approaches (such as Dyer's) that attempt to understand the consequences of media objects from a 'reading' of their internal textual characteristics are a mistake. He refers to this mistake as the *fallacy of internalism*.

According to Thompson, we need to go 'outside' those products (and indeed their production) to examine the complex processes that are likely to be involved in their consumption. Unless we develop more sophisticated forms of inquiry that help us to reveal the different investments that members of the audience have in celebrities, such textual readings are unlikely to take us very far on their own. The idea of 'empirical' audience studies is actually built upon such a view. For example, while Adorno's work on fascism still represents a warning from history, it is noticeable that he studies the texts of fascist speeches to make assumptions about the audience. This is a view that has come under increasing scrutiny from media and cultural studies. Many audience analysts in media studies believe that a particular author cannot simply read off the 'meaning' of a celebrity or star (in the way we tried to do earlier with James Dean, following Dyer's approach). Instead, they claim, we should seek to uncover the different ways in which diverse members of the audience make sense of celebrities. The question thus becomes not so much what celebrities do to us, but what we *do with* celebrities.

3.2 A study of female audiences

As an example of such an approach, we shall look at a study of cinema audiences by Jackie Stacey (1994), a British feminist film historian. Her work seeks to understand the specific pleasure and engagements of British cinema audiences in the 1940s and 1950s. The people who participated in her study went to the cinema two or three times a week, this activity being their main form of leisure. Also notable about this period was the ways in which women from lower-middle class and working-class backgrounds were targeted as the main consumers of motion pictures. Stacey's study focuses on female spectatorship and it was generated empirically out of 350 letters she received from people telling her of their experiences of cinema-going during this period.

Stacey's work is important not only because of the emphasis she places upon the audience in the context of the study of film, but also because she locates her work in a tradition of media analysis that explores 'female spectatorship'. In this tradition there is great emphasis upon how an analysis of film texts can help us to understand the way in which a film constructs sexual difference. The concern is less with what female members of the audience experience on a trip to the cinema than on how masculine and feminine 'subject positions' are constructed by a film text. For example, one important argument in early studies of spectatorship, which for a while dominated feminist film studies, was that the use of the 'male gaze' by male characters, directed at female characters, determined the pleasure that was available to the viewers of a particular film. Women, it was argued, are 'objectified' by the gaze of the masculine characters within the film. The spectator, meanwhile, is offered a kind of voyeuristic pleasure in looking at men looking at women.

However, Stacey argues that what is missing from the spectatorship approach is not only 'real' audiences, as opposed to assumptions about spectators, but also analysis about how people might read particular film texts 'against the grain', that is, against the 'dominant' or 'preferred meaning' of the film (see Hall, 1980, p.134; and Chapter 2, Section 2). For Stacey, the spectatorship approach is wrong to assume that women have to adopt the dominant masculine position offered by the text in order to gain pleasure from looking at female stars. Stacey wants to explore the more fluid possibilities of viewing the text that might be available to female members of the audience. In particular, she is interested in exploring the homoerotic pleasures that are available to female spectators. In this way, rather than attempting to read people's subjectivities from film texts themselves, Stacey broadens the argument to include the pleasures of the cinema.

What did Stacey learn from her research? Overwhelmingly Stacey's respondents reported that a trip to the cinema offered the possibility of an escape into a glamorous world. This was the case not only in the way in which they constructed their relationship with the stars on the screen in the 1940s and 1950s, but also through their memories of the cinema-going experience. For many a night out at the cinema offered a sense of glamour, and an appreciation of luxury and the exotic, in an era of austerity. The pleasures of the cinema were not only visual, but engaged other senses as well. Many respondents reported enjoying the relative plush and warmth of the cinema compared to the world outside. There were also various pleasures associated with being part of the crowd. A trip to the cinema (or the 'pictures') depended on a shared sense of intimacy and community with other members of the audience. Going to the cinema was thus a way of escaping from the anxiety about losing family members during the war, more mundane domestic concerns, and a world of shortage and 'making do'.

However, the relationship between members of the audience and the stars on the screen was complex. Stacey argues that the most common reason given for the choice of a particular film was the specific star who was appearing in a 'picture'. In this, Hollywood stars were preferred over their British counterparts. This seemingly had less to do with the economic dominance of films from the US, and more because Hollywood offered a contrast to ordinary lives dominated by loss and rationing. What was experienced pleasurably was the 'distance' between the glamorous world of the stars and the everyday pain of the lives of the audience. In Stacey's (1994, p.117) words, it is the stark contrast between the world of the stars and the spectator that 'provide[s] the possibility for the spectator to leave her world temporarily and become part of the star's world'. A successful trip to the cinema depended upon the transformations made possible by an everyday magic. The fantasy engaged in by the audience did not just act as a compensation for the world outside the cinema, but allowed the possibility for the audience to generate fantasised, imaginary selves. A visit to the cinema could become part of pleasurable and utopian experience.

Stacey's account stresses the intense feelings of adoration and devotion that were evident among female members of the audience. However, despite the 'other worldly' nature of the stars, spectators regularly sought to take on aspects of their identity. So an intense relationship with a particular star or stars offered fantasies of personal transformation. By bringing the star or stars 'into the self', many of Stacey's respondents said that they were able to take on their attributes and characteristics. This could lead to an increased sense of courage, confidence or individuality on the part of spectators.

Reading 4.1, from Stacey's book, will give you some indication of the evidence she draws on.

Reading 4.1 Activity

Now read the following extracts from Jackie Stacey, 'Aspiration and inspiration' (Reading 4.1). When you have read it through, make a note of the different fantasies, according to Stacey, that stars could activate for their audiences.

Reading 4.1

Jackie Stacey, 'Aspiration and inspiration'

In this [...] section, the processes analysed involve the spectator's identity more centrally. Here the star's identity is written about [...] in relation to the desire for transformation of the spectator's identity. The discourses through which the star is remembered, then, are ones which centre on the feminine identity of the spectators [...]

In some examples the relationship between star and spectator is articulated through the recognition of an immutable difference between star and spectator:

> Hollywood stars in the roles they depicted were all the things we'd have liked to have been, wearing glamorous clothes and jewels we had no chance of acquiring and doing so many wonderful things we knew we would never have the nerve to do – even given the opportunity ... Bette Davis was the epitome of what we would like to be, but knew we never could!
>
> Norah Turner

Yet here the desire to move across that difference and become more like the stars is expressed, even if it is accompanied by the impossibility of its fulfilment. [...] The distance between the spectator and her ideal produces a kind of longing which offers fantasies of transformed identities. 'The cinema took you into the realm of fantasy and what you as a person would like to be and do' (Anon).

These desires to become more like the stars occur on several levels. Many of them are predictably articulated through the discourse of glamour. Stars offer ideals of feminine appearance:

> I finally kept with Joan Crawford – every typist's dream of how they'd like to look.
>
> May Ross

> And of course her (Betty Grable's) clothes – how could a young girl not want to look like that?
>
> Sheila Wright

> Joan Bennett – not so much for her acting, I can't even remember her films. I just thought she was gorgeous. The star I would most like to look like.
>
> Joyce Lewis

> We liked to think we were like them, but of course, we couldn't match any of the female stars for looks or clothes. It was nice to have them as role models though!
>
> Valerie Channell

Not surprisingly, stars serve a normative function to the extent that they are often read as role models, contributing to the construction of ideals of feminine attractiveness circulating at that time. Stars were variously referred to as 'role models', 'someone to emulate' and 'the epitome of what every woman should be'. Spectators often felt 'unattractive', 'dowdy', 'plump' and 'gangly' by comparison. Stars are remembered through a discourse of feminine glamour in which ideals of feminine appearance (slim, white, young and even-featured) were established and in comparison to which many spectators felt inadequate.

Successful physical attractiveness also signifies successful romantic conclusions:

> Although I wished to look like a different star each week depending on what film I saw, I think my favourite was Rita Hayworth, I always imagined if I could look like her I could toss my red hair into the wind ... and meet the man of my dreams.
>
> Rene Arter

Figure 4.4 *Joan Crawford*

Figure 4.5 *Rita Hayworth*

Furthermore, glamour is linked to wealth and property, as the following example demonstrates:

> my enjoyment of going to the pictures was my way of imagining myself one day going somewhere equally lovely and being able to wear lovely gowns and meet a rich handsome man and have a big house with servants, especially when I had seen a colour film!
>
> Jean Forshaw

Thus Hollywood stars function as role models encouraging desire for feminine 'attractiveness', attachment to a man and possession of property (and even servants!). This encouraged traditional forms of aspiration among women whose lives were very unlike anything they saw on the Hollywood screen.

However, star glamour was understood not only in terms of appearance, but also as signifying confidence, sophistication and self-assurance, which were perceived by female spectators as desirable and inspirational:

> Maureen O'Hara seemed to me, a teenager, the type of person I would have liked to be as she was the complete opposite of me. Her fiery beauty and nature, and the way she handled situations in her films were magical to me. The same applies to Marilyn Monroe. I was a shorthand typist-cum-secretary; life was rather run of the mill, the lifestyles they portrayed were something we could only dream about.
>
> Brenda Blackman

What is interesting here is that it is not only the 'beauty' which was admired, but also 'the way she handled situations', suggesting a kind of ability and confidence in the world which the spectator herself felt she lacked:

> I liked seeing strong, capable and independent types of female characters mostly because I wished to be like them.
>
> Joan Clifford
>
> Likening myself to women who portrayed characters I would have liked to have been or had the courage to have been.
>
> Mrs P. McDonald
>
> I think I admired the ones I would like to have been like and considered myself uninteresting, being quiet and shy.
>
> Anon

Thus the courage, confidence and independence of feminine stars is aspired to by spectators who saw themselves as unable to enjoy such admirable qualities.

Some female stars, such as Bette Davis, Joan Crawford and Katharine Hepburn, were frequently referred to as representing images of power and confidence. These were frequent favourites because they offered spectators fantasies of power outside their own experience:

> We liked stars who were most different to ourselves and Katharine Hepburn, with her self-assured romps through any situation was one of them. We were youngsters at the time, and were anything but self-confident, and totally lacking in sophistication, so, naturally, Bette Davis took the other pedestal. She could be a real 'bitch', without turning a hair, and quelled her leading men with a raised eyebrow and a sneer at the corners of her mouth.
>
> Norah Turner
>
> Bette Davis ... was great, I loved how she walked across the room in her films, she seemed to have a lot of confidence and she had a look of her own, as I think a lot of the female stars had at that time.
>
> Anon

Figure 4.6 *Katharine Hepburn*

Figure 4.7 *Bette Davis*

Powerful female stars often played characters in punishing patriarchal narratives, where the woman is either killed off, or married, or both, but these spectators do not seem to select this aspect of their films to write about. Instead, the qualities of confidence and power are remembered as offering female spectators the pleasure of participation in qualities they themselves lacked and desired.

Again, the age difference between the star and the younger fans is central here, and stars provide ideals of femininity for adolescent women in the audience who are preoccupied with attaining adult femininity:

> Doris Day ... seemed to epitomise the kind of person, who with luck, I as a child could aspire to be.
>
> Betty Cole

> I favoured stars I could identify with – romantic, adventurous, glamorous, strong minded – all the things I hoped to become 'when I grew up'.
>
> M. Palin

Thus female stars represented not only ideals of feminine glamour in terms of appearance, but also a mature femininity which was a source of fascination to younger spectators. Stars were envied for their confidence and their capabilities in the fictional worlds of Hollywood cinema.

These examples demonstrate not simply the desire to overcome the gap between spectator and star, but a fantasy of possible movement between the two identities, from the spectator to the star:

> I preferred stars who were unlike women I knew. They were better dressed and looked much more attractive. They gave me the ambition to do more for myself.
>
> Anon

Hollywood stars can thus be seen as offering more than simple role models of sexual attractiveness (though clearly they offered this too!). However, they were also remembered as offering female spectators a source of fantasy of a more powerful and confident self:

> I think everyone needs an inspiration or aspiration. Some of the stars I liked because they were down to earth, but they usually became something quite different in their films, making one feel that the unattainable could be reached.
>
> Marie Burgess

[...] I have discussed processes of spectatorship which involve negotiating the difference between the star and the spectator in various ways. [...] what can be seen clearly is that these processes of spectatorship involve distinct relations between self and ideal. [...] In (this) section, the desire to transform the self and become more like the ideal were explored. [...] the boundary between self and ideal is [...] fluid and relational. [...]

Reading source

Stacey, 1994, pp.151–9 ■ ■ ■

Activity 4.3

Can you think of similar examples of identification with stars from your own experience? How generally true do you think such processes of identification are? What is your view of such identification: is it a positive feature of audience activity as Stacey suggests? ■ ■ ■

One obvious objection to Stacey's approach from an Adornian and Horkheimian perspective is that Stacey is describing a form of mere copying. In Adorno and Horkheimian's terms, the intense identification with stars is an attempt to develop a form of 'pseudo-individuality' rather than a more 'authentic' individualism (1979, p.128; p.154; see Chapter 1, Section 4). Surely, we might object, this is just another example of how people in consumer societies try to take on the 'pose' of individuality by buying consumer products in the marketplace.

For Stacey this argument is not only inaccurate, distorting more subtle aspects of experience, but it is also potentially – a problem for her – elitist. She asserts that the pleasurable forms of identification with a star's image are active rather than passive processes. For example, for many female spectators in her study, identification with a particular star became linked to a desire to change their outward appearance. Stacey interprets this not as a form of passivity but, in the context of 1940s' and 1950s' Britain, as a form of rebellion. In British society during this period for a woman to reconstruct the details of her appearance (for example, dyeing her hair) through identification with a certain star was to run up against societal codes of 'respectable' femininity. Hence, rather than the overtly negative reading evident in Adorno's writing, Stacey argues that to understand the relationship of stars with audiences we need to explore how identity is regulated by certain codes and discourses. For women, the key site of transformation in a consumer culture is the body, given that women are judged by their appearance in a way that is still not the case for men. Hence, the subversive nature of female consumers of cinema culture depends upon women's ability to challenge the ways that their bodies are regulated by the culture of the time. What Stacey calls 'rebellious' is the capacity of female spectators to break with the prevailing dominant norms. Obviously we need to be aware that changing your hair colour is not necessarily a subversive practice in itself. However, Stacey offers a more nuanced and positive reading of people's fascination with charismatic stars and celebrities than is evident in Adorno's (1991) critical theory, and one based on interaction with members of the audience.

People's interest in stars and celebrities could well be a way of escaping the confines of everyday life and establishing a more positive sense of personal and collective identity. However, it could also be that Stacey over-identifies with the lives of the people she is researching. It is very difficult to conduct this kind of face-to-face audience research and not have some sympathy with the people one is researching. Yet, we could equally argue that Stacey adopts a theoretical framework that is both more sensitive to questions of gender (mostly absent from Adorno and Horkheimer's accounts of media reception) and alive to some of the complexities of the experience of ordinary consumers in ways that are absent from critical theory. So, rather than simply assuming that the subjectivity of the audience can be 'read off' from different media texts and consumer products, Stacey seeks to engage with the audience in a more concrete fashion.

4 Fans as 'ideal' audiences in media and cultural studies

Jackie Stacey's work is representative of a shift in studies of stardom and celebrity towards a much more optimistic interpretation of the audience, based in many cases on interviews with, or letters from, fans. To an important degree, the audience – depending on a host of contextualising factors such as gender or class – uses the media for its own, perhaps unexpected, ends. Much of the first research of this kind was undertaken by researchers associated with the emerging 'discipline' of cultural studies in the 1980s. Some of the most controversial work on audiences in cultural studies concerns fandom and is clearly relevant to our survey of different approaches to the relationship between media, celebrity and audiences.

The claim that much of this work seeks to subvert relates to the view that only 'abnormal' or 'psychologically disturbed' people form intense relationships with celebrities. It is easy to see where this notion comes from. Much of the media's reporting of fans represents them as being dangerous and out of control. Fans are seen as stalkers creeping into the bedrooms of their favourite stars, or as lonely obsessives who spend a lifetime hunting down trivial artefacts connected in some way with their idols. Much of the cultural studies literature has sought to argue that this creates not only a misleading picture, but one that makes it difficult to admit our own fandom to others. Fans may then want to keep their enthusiasms to themselves (unless they know it is safe to do otherwise) for fear of being labelled mad, bad or simply dangerous. To be a fan is a fairly ordinary phenomenon. We all know people (if not ourselves) who are fans of football, soap operas, cult television shows or stars of cinema and popular music. Being a fan means that we follow the careers of particular celebrities with an intensity that is less evident in other cultural arenas. Usually being a fan means it 'really' matters to us if our favourite team wins or loses, whether our favourite band has entered the charts at number 1, or that the television schedules have just dropped a favourite show. Consequently, much of the work that has been done in this area has sought to avoid turning people who identify with celebrities into the opposite of the norm, an 'other'.

If being a fan of a celebrity or group of celebrities is a much more ordinary experience than we usually like to admit, then how might we build a different model of interpretation that steers clear of making sweeping assumptions (accounts for the difference of fans) and make sense of a wide range of fan activity? Next we will look at some of the work of the British cultural studies writer, John Fiske, and others, who sought to build on these ideas.

4.1 Fans as active audiences: the work of John Fiske

John Fiske's work on audiences in media and cultural studies is well known, and has attracted a great deal of interest and controversy. He is not necessarily representative of cultural studies as a whole, but he typifies the association of cultural studies with very optimistic readings of audiences, and fans especially. Fiske argues that earlier waves of theorising overstated the passivity of the media audience. We have already seen how this has indeed been a problem that has been associated with the Frankfurt School tradition of critical theory and earlier forms of film studies. Instead of simply assuming that audiences are relatively passive in their adoration of stars and celebrities, Fiske wants to demonstrate the falsity of this view by drawing on his own and other people's empirical work. He seeks to demonstrate that audience passivity is actually a prejudice amongst elitist academics who have little interaction with popular culture. Fans, then, with their particularly strong forms of attachment to celebrities, can be seen as ideal examples of an active audience. Before we look at some of the case studies Fiske produced, we will examine what he says about fan cultures more generally.

For John Fiske (1991) fans can be characterised in the following interrelated ways:

- To be a fan involves a pleasurable reworking of the texts and forms of visual culture that the media of mass communication make commonly available. Fans are not so much passive in this process, but by interacting with media cultures produce new meanings and understandings.

- While Fiske is careful not to 'pathologise' fans (that is, to treat them as if they were suffering from sickness), he distinguishes them from 'normal' audiences. Fans typically exhibit forms of enthusiasm, intensity and excitement that are missing from more mundane interactions with media cultures.

- Fans are typically associated with forms of commercial culture that the dominant value system deems to be unworthy. Apologists for forms of culture associated with the more highly educated classes traditionally view fan activity through a sceptical lens, which typically suggests it is a lowly, base and generally non-elevated set of activities.

- For Fiske, fans are usually associated with the tastes of disempowered social groups. Fans are usually people who have low levels of educational attainment and are excluded along the lines of class, 'race' and gender. As you saw in Chapter 2, Section 5, it is the aspect of celebrity that supplies audiences with unofficial forms of knowledge which makes it so pleasurable. Similarly, according to Fiske, it is not considered 'the done thing' in educated circles to pay too much attention to the cultures of celebrity. Being caught reading a copy of

Heat magazine or *Hello!* can supposedly threaten your social status and lead to feelings of shame and embarrassment. This is because 'official' forms of culture like to look down upon supposedly more 'ephemeral' cultures associated with celebrity (see Chapter 2, Section 5)

In making this last point, Fiske draws upon an argument that is often attributed to the French sociologist Pierre Bourdieu (1930–2002). While Bourdieu did not write on the subject of celebrity and little on the media, his work is important in understanding issues of taste and value in relation to media products and activities.

One of Bourdieu's (1984) key insights in this context is what he calls 'the arbitrariness of culture'. By this he means that there is no intrinsic reason why educated tastes, aesthetic preferences and cultural judgements should be taken as indicative of high culture, as better than any other forms of culture. The love of abstract art, classical music and other cultural styles function as a form of social distinction. What a society takes to be culturally valuable is, for Bourdieu, largely determined by the social structure. So, apparently disinterested practices such as the appreciation of a fine wine, a visit to an art gallery or indeed a preference for Stravinsky over Chopin are used to gain what Bourdieu (1986) calls 'cultural capital'. The idea here is that just as some groups can gain more economic capital than others, social groups can also gain knowledge and skills in the realm of culture. Just as the upper middle classes have more economic capital than the lower middle class and the working class, they also have cultural capital. These knowledges and skills are embodied in particular ways of speaking, standing, walking, thinking and feeling. So, the experience of going to an art gallery can be a much more intimidating experience for a working-class person than an upper middle-class person. Taste, for Bourdieu, is part of a battle over distinction, over efforts to *differentiate* ourselves from others. This is a battle that, importantly, can take place within social classes as well as across them. Fiske uses Bourdieu's argument about cultural capital to show how celebrities are used by fans and audiences to create distinctions between groups.

Fiske's argument about fan cultures goes further than the suggestion that an interest in celebrity on the part of audiences is connected to questions of status. In particular, as indicated above, he wants to emphasise the active rather than passive nature of fandom. The main way in which fandom works is as a form of 'in-group solidarity' among those who participate within a particular fan group, and a way of marking themselves off from the rest of the world or 'official culture'. To be a fan then is to mark your distinction from non-fans or other fan groups, and to establish yourself against a wider community.

However, as Fiske is well aware, all communities produce formal and informal rules. Indeed many fan communities, despite being low in 'official' cultural capital, establish their own hierarchies and alternative forms of cultural capital. There are ways in which fans can increase their esteem and status within a particular fan community, which are not recognised and indeed may hardly be understood, by those outside that community. This might involve being knowledgeable about a particular sports team or celebrity, or by running an 'unofficial' website, or indeed helping to run a fan club or producing a newsletter. However, of all these different activities, it is the accumulation of fan knowledge that is most important. Those who have expertise within a fan community are most likely to gain respect from other fans. Fans, therefore, are often buffs who avidly collect a diverse range of material from videos to magazine articles, and from paper clippings to 'unofficial' photographs and bootlegs. In other words, even though the activity of fans may lack 'official' cultural capital, becoming a fan can be a way of accumulating 'unofficial' capital while having fun. So, for Fiske, there is something excessive in fan behaviour that marks them out from 'ordinary' consumers. By this Fiske does not mean that they lack the capacity to discriminate (actually they are highly selective), but that fans often collect a wide range of cultural and symbolic forms and objects which, while 'unique' to the fan, may be 'meaningless' to outsiders. For example, as part of current research, I have recently been interviewing fans of David Bowie. I have found that many Bowie fans collect mundane objects that others would not invest with the same importance. These might be ticket stubs, rare records, old concert programmes, obscure artwork and magazine articles. The distinctiveness of these objects lies not in the individual objects themselves, but in the significance the collection has for a particular fan. This is where Fiske's views come back in. Cultural taste is arbitrary, in that the value of objects is not internal to them, but is attributed, on the basis of social experience, and the attempt by audiences to distinguish themselves from other social groups.

Building on this, we will now explore a somewhat different issue in Fiske's (1991) work, which is that, against views which see audiences as passive, he sees some members of the audience – especially fans – as so active that they become producers in themselves. The activity of fans can be said to be productive in three ways.

■ *Semiotic productivity* This is the fans' capacity to make meanings and construct their identity by interacting with the products made commonly available by commercial cultures.

■ *Enunciative productivity* The circulation of in-group meanings within a particular fan community is a pleasurable way to make collective identities. This form of community might exist online in internet discussion groups, through face-to-face meetings, or by being at a concert or sporting event.

- *Textual productivity* Fan communities commonly produce a range of texts that are not intended to become part of the official economy. This form of productivity is produced specifically for circulation among people who share similar passions and tastes. These might include the production of fan web pages or indeed fanzines.

This notion of audience 'productivity', especially among fans, is one of the factors that allows Fiske to say that 'popular culture is made by the people, not produced by the culture industry' (Fiske, 1989a, p.24), a view that you may remember is part of the populist perspective discussed in Chapter 1. To be considered popular, therefore, commodities have to be mass produced for economic return and potentially open to the subversive readings of the people. For Fiske, once a person has purchased the new Madonna CD from the local music store, the product has become detached from the strategies of capitalism. The music of Madonna is not simply a standardised product that can be purchased through the institutions of global capitalism, but is a cultural resource of everyday life. The act of consumption always entails a new production of meaning.

For Fiske (1989a, 1989b) the circulation of meaning requires us to study three levels of textuality, but it is also important to study the specific relations between them (see the earlier discussion of categorising texts in Chapter 2, Section 3). First, there are the cultural forms that are produced alongside the new Madonna album to create the idea of a media event. These can include concerts, books, posters and videos. At the next level, there is a variety of media talk in popular magazines and newspapers, television programmes and radio shows, all offering critical commentary upon Madonna. The final level of textuality, the one to which Fiske claims to be most attentive, involves the ways in which Madonna becomes part of our everyday life. According to Fiske (1989b), Madonna's career was launched by a rock video of an early song called 'Lucky Star'. She became established in 1985 as a cultural icon through a series of successful albums and singles, the film *Desperately Seeking Susan* (USA, dir. Seidelman, 1985), nude shots that appeared in *Penthouse* and *Playboy* magazines, as well as the successful marketing of a certain 'look'. Fiske argues that Madonna symbolically plays with traditional stereotypes of women – the virgin and the whore – in order to subtly subvert patriarchal meanings (see Figure 4.8). That is, Madonna uses textual devices (see Chapter 2) that 'destabilise' or challenge these traditional representations of women. Fiske accounts for Madonna's success by arguing that she is an 'open' text rather than a 'closed' one – she can be read in many ways, rather than strongly inviting a particular 'preferred' reading. She is able to challenge her fans to reinvent their own sexual identities out of the cultural resources that she and patriarchal capitalism provides. In the final analysis, Madonna's popularity is not simply a consequence of her promotion by the media industries, but of her attempts to forge her own identity within a male-dominant culture, which have a certain relevance for her fans.

While Fiske draws from a range of cultural theory, most notably semiotics and post-structuralism, the work of the French writer Michel de Certeau (1984) has a particular resonance for his approach. For de Certeau, popular culture is best defined as the operations performed upon texts, rather than the actual domains of the texts themselves. Everyday life has to operate within the spaces that have been carved out by the powerful. To read a fashion magazine, listen to a punk album, put on a soccer supporter's scarf, or pin up a picture of Madonna, is to discover a way of using common culture that is not strictly prescribed by its makers. The act of consumption is part of what de Certeau calls the 'tactics' of the weak. This converts disciplinary and instrumental time into that which is free and creative. For instance, the practice of writing a love letter while at work is, for de Certeau, a means of stealing time from an instrumental activity and diverting it into a more sensuous pursuit. Similarly, in terms of media audiences, while the practices of the powerful dominate the production of cultural forms and regulate the spaces of their reception, the actual reading processes of the 'weak', the acts of reception themselves, elude strategies of direct control.

Following de Certeau, Fiske dispenses with the notion of the 'preferred reading' found in media studies (see Chapter 2). Both Fiske and de Certeau are keen to distance themselves from cultural theories, such as those of Adorno and Horkheimer (1979), which assume that through emulating a 'product' the consumer becomes like it. Instead, for Fiske and de Certeau, consumers make the product more like themselves: they actively do *something new* with it. This means that our interactions with stars and celebrities are located in forms of self-empowerment and our capacity to engage in the production of meanings that are different from those intended by producers.

Activity 4.4

Make notes on the following questions:

- What do you think of Fiske's views?
- Do you agree that fans of particular celebrities are engaging in active consumption in the way that Fiske describes? ■ ■ ■

Fiske, drawing on de Certeau, suggests a positive reading of celebrity in that it provides the weak with resources to struggle against various forms of disempowerment. Yet it could be argued that this captures only some of the features of a celebrity-oriented media, and ignores others. In the rest of this section we will look at accounts of celebrity that problematise Fiske's views, but from within a cultural studies perspective.

(a)   (b)

Figure 4.8 *Madonna in 1985 (a) and in 1990 (b)*

4.2 Criticisms of John Fiske

A different account of Madonna that is both supportive and critical of Fiske has been developed by Douglas Kellner (1995). He argues that Madonna is not so much the site of *resistance* as of *contradiction*. Kellner concedes that Madonna's shifting persona or image, which in Fiske's view serves to destabilise dominant representations of gender and sexuality, can indeed act as a form of female empowerment. However, Kellner goes on to say that Madonna's experiments with gender bending and transgressive sexual identities have to be seen in the broader context of the media industries. Ultimately her skillful manipulation of image and culture is emblematic of mainstream consumer narcissism, meaning that in modern consumer society the individual self or the 'new you' can be purchased, ready made, from the shelves of the capitalist-dominated fashion industry. Taking a view similar to the cultural decline critics discussed in Chapter 1, Kellner is concerned that a narcissistic concern for image is privileged over alternative forms of politics that emphasise the role of commitment and concern for the well-being of others. While Madonna exhibits a radicalism in terms of the politics of gender and sexuality, ultimately she promotes a concern for the cultivation of the 'surface' of the individual, rather than responsibility for the wider community or the common good. Madonna in this regard is both politically radical (subverting images of male dominance) and conservative (reproducing dominant ideas about consumer culture and capitalism).

Another criticism that could be made of the work of Fiske is that his enthusiastic account of fan culture (and Fiske was only one prominent advocate of a celebration of the activity of fans in cultural studies in the 1980s and 1990s) neglects to analyse the more ordinary aspects of popular culture. This is a point made by the Dutch writer, Joke Hermes (1995). She criticises the overemphasis of earlier media studies on the text, and identifies what she calls 'the fallacy of meaningfulness' (Hermes, 1995, p.16), which is the assumption that all forms of popular media carry significant meanings. Her work is concerned with the relationship between everyday life, women's magazines and ordinary readers. Hermes insists on the everyday and mundane character of magazine reading for the majority of her readers (accessed via 80 in-depth interviews). Magazines are 'leafed through' during gaps in readers' everyday routines; they are 'easily put down' rather than invested with any deep significance. Magazine reading emerges as 'a low-priority means of spending leisure time or unoccupied minutes' (Hermes, 1995, p.20) rather than having any greater cultural or political significance. Therefore, we might argue that Fiske but also Kellner presume an overly neat fit between their readings of Madonna and her global audiences.

Another way of understanding Hermes's interpretation is that, because the media of mass communication are so regularly full of celebrities, most of us adopt a blasé attitude towards mediated celebrities, most of the time. The German sociologist Georg Simmel (1858–1918) observed that the blasé attitude developed within urban cultures at the turn of the nineteenth century as a way of dealing with the 'intensification of nervous stimulation' (1903/1997, p.175) connected to everyday life in the city. According to Simmel, in urban cultures people have to contend with a rush of visual experiences, changing fashions and arresting images, and their blasé attitude emerges from this over stimulation of the senses. Perhaps Hermes captured some of this attitude in her work? 'To be blasé', argued Simmel (1903/1997), is to adopt the disposition that 'no one object deserves preference over another'. Indeed, given the saturation coverage of celebrities by the mass media and the music industry, and through sports promotions, it would be surprising if the audience did not adopt this disposition occasionally. Such factors easily become displaced in overly enthusiastic accounts of commercial pleasures. Audiences surely do not always 'resist' in the ways that have been identified by Fiske. However, perhaps we should also avoid pushing Simmel's argument too far. There is plenty of evidence that, in certain contexts, media audiences still respond enthusiastically to popular celebrities.

This point about the banality of much media consumption allows us to make some further reflections on Stacey's study (discussed in Section 3), and on the growth of celebrity as a phenomenon. Stacey deals with the most 'glamorous' and powerful of entertainment stars. It could be argued that 'celebrities' are much more mundane beings. Indeed many of the people who participated in Stacey's study remarked that the stars and celebrities of today seemed more 'ordinary' compared to the worlds of glamour they occupied in years gone by. While this view is undoubtedly tinged with feelings of nostalgia, many have suggested that contemporary 'celebrity culture' is indeed a response to change (see the discussion of the 'cultural decline' position in Chapter 1).

With the expansion of media cultures over the past twenty or thirty years we could argue that there are increased possibilities for many of becoming at least a minor celebrity – a view expressed by the democratic-populists as discussed in Chapter 1. The multiplicity of television channels and magazines, and the development of 24-hour broadcasting has meant that working in the media sector has become a career option for increasing numbers of people. In the context of our discussion, however, it might mean that *audience members* are now increasingly likely to perceive themselves as potential stars and celebrities, rather than being content to admire others from afar (see Chapter 1, Section 1). This points to the possibility of a changing relationship between media, celebrity and the audiences who spend most of their time doing the 'looking' or listening. The development of internet sites centring on particular celebrities has seemingly given many fans a sense of intimate involvement (for example, online discussions with other fans or a with a celebrity). However, we need to be clear that most of the audience are still unlikely to become either stars or celebrities. Most ordinary people's relationship to celebrities involves reading magazines, watching television and attending the cinema. But the proliferation of celebrity raises some important questions about the mundane quality of audience experiences of celebrity, compared with the intense forms of identification analysed by Stacey. In her work on women's magazines, Hermes (1999) finds very little evidence that people actually identify with the celebrities they read about. What is much more significant is the way that celebrities become woven into certain narratives and discourses. This takes us into the fourth and final view of media, celebrity and audiences that we will look at in this chapter.

5   A constructionist view of celebrity

In the previous section, through the use of Kellner's work on Madonna, I introduced the idea of trying to form an understanding of the ways people respond ambivalently to celebrities, and popular culture more generally. If Adorno's critical theory sought to understand the way that stars and celebrities are part of a culture of domination, then it seems that many within cultural studies have simply reversed these ideas and assumptions. The idea that the relationship we construct with stars and celebrities is either negative or positive seems too sweeping. In this section, I will look further at ways in which we might go beyond the choice between optimistic and pessimistic readings of the relationship between audiences and celebrities – and between audiences and the media more generally. I also reflect on research methods, to explore the different methodologies and relationships that are formed between researchers and participants in their studies.

5.1 Defining constructionism

A constructionist view of the audience and celebrity dispenses with the notion that either stars or celebrities have 'definite' effects on the subjectivity of the audience or that we simply incorporate them in any unified way into our everyday lives. Rather, it views celebrities less as role models, and pays more attention to the ways they become constructed and reconstructed in language and discourses. Pertti Alasuutari (1999) has argued that such an approach to celebrity would need to begin from the position that media audiences are constantly shifting through a multitude of discourses and positions in respect of media cultures. This means that individual members of the audience at different times of the day could indeed occupy positions which are similar to those described by critical theory and cultural studies. In particular, those taking a constructionist view are concerned to map out the different relations that audiences have with celebrity media texts. This allows researchers to be more open to the idea that ambivalent positions can be taken up by members of an audience for a celebrity, or for any media product. The argument is, then, that we need to move away from the notion that the audience is permanently fixed into positions of domination or resistance. Here, we might try to understand not whether the audience resists dominant media messages or complies with them, but how the audience is positioned within a number of complex and competing discourses. (The meaning of 'discourse' varies in different areas of the humanities and social science, but in this context, and in much media studies work, it refers to a way of talking and writing about an aspect of life or society that at the same time defines it in a certain way. See Chapter 1, p.25–7.) Within a single interview, for example, a focus group or interview participant might see celebrity as a way of selling products for the media industries, and then move between a blasé attitude and more enthusiastic forms of identification when talking about particular stars and celebrities. So, for the view I am developing here, the old question as to whether audiences are active or dominated by the flow of media cultures is overly restrictive.

Here the argument will try to capture the contradictory forms of thinking and feeling about celebrity.

5.2 The case of men's lifestyle magazines

To illustrate this, let us turn to some research that I conducted with colleagues into men's lifestyle magazines (Jackson et al., 2001) which looked at the production and consumption of men's magazines and included interviews with editors, exploration of magazine content, and focus group interviews with mostly young men. Focusing on a range of titles from *GQ* to *Loaded* and from *FHM* to *Attitude* we set out to examine the ways in which the magazines and their consumption could be related to wider questions of masculinity and of changes in men's position in society. In particular, we examined the different discourses (ways of constructing the objects of masculinity and feminity) and fantasies that the magazines make available to their readers.

Reading 4.2 Activity

Now read the following extract from Peter Jackson, Nick Stevenson and Kate Brooks, 'Making sense of men's magazines' (Reading 4.2). As you read, make some notes on how the discussion of audience responses to men's magazines differ from the previous approaches we have discussed.

Reading 4.2

Peter Jackson, Nick Stevenson and Kate Brooks, 'Making sense of men's magazines'

'Honesty'

Several groups distinguished *Loaded* from the rest of the magazines, claiming that, while others pretended to be sophisticated, cultured and intelligent, *Loaded* was 'more blatant', with 'no pretensions' (Islington professionals). Magazines like *GQ* were described as 'arty' or 'aspirational' (for people with 'lashings of dosh'), presenting a superficial or glossy image of the 'new man'. By contrast, *Loaded* was more 'honest': 'a celebration of the unacceptable face of men' (Pimlico graduates). Even among those who preferred 'classier' magazines such as *Arena*, with 'more cultural integrity', a contrast could still be drawn between magazines such as *GQ* and *Esquire*, 'dressing themselves up in a glossy cover', and *Loaded*, which was 'a bit more basic' (London journalists). Similarly, those who found *Arena* too highbrow ('pseudo-arty'), like the Sunday broadsheets, would read

Loaded 'just for a laugh', as they did the tabloids (Turnpike Lane graduates).

Some groups were sceptical about *Loaded*'s way of addressing its readers, seeing it as 'manipulative' (Stoke Newington media professionals) or as appealing to the 'lowest common denominator' (London counsellors). For the majority of respondents, however, *Loaded*'s blatant emphasis on women, sport and entertainment was a welcome contrast to the 'airs and graces' of the more style-conscious magazines: 'They make no qualms about it ... they're not hypocritical' (Bristol students). Other groups also spoke about the 'honest and open view' of 'shameless' magazines like *Loaded* which don't feel any need to justify themselves (Manchester lecturers), celebrating 'a kind of freedom to ... shout and be kind of loud and get pissed' (Stoke Newington media professionals).

Loaded's founding editor James Brown was singled out for praise by many readers. Unlike the other magazines, whose editors had to strive for success in a calculated manner, James Brown was said to embody the magazine's values in a more natural way (recalling our discussion of 'authenticity' in Chapter 3). Although he studiously cultivated this image (via biographical material on the *UpLoaded* website and in media interviews, for example), many readers appeared to take the image at face value: 'He seemed to live and breathe it ... in an honest way' (Bristol musicians and artists). Whether Brown's popular reputation has survived his latest business exploits remains to be seen: in May 2000, he successfully floated his own publishing company ('I Feel Good Holdings plc') on the Alternative Investment Market at a valuation of £10 million. Describing his publishing philosophy as 'trying to unite the disciplines I learned at Condé Nast with the editorial freedom of *Loaded*', he realised a £5 million profit before the first issue of his latest magazine *Hot Dog* had reached the news-stands (*The Guardian*, 22 May 2000).

'Naturalness'

Many of our focus group participants argued that the image of the lad was a more natural form of masculinity than the contrived image of the new man which it replaced as a dominant media construction during the 1990s. The magazines were welcomed as promoting an image of masculinity that was more natural in at least two senses: more authentic (true to men's real selves) and less contrived (unlike images of the new man). The idea that the new man was a media fiction was widely shared: 'The new man went too far [... he was] unrealistic [and] didn't exist except on television' (Sheffield 18-year-olds); he was 'a fiction created by Richard and Judy [day-time TV presenters]' (London journalists); 'all about image' (Bristol lecturers);

'a mythical creation [...] completely unrealistic and artificial [...] I think the media makes a lot of it up' (London counsellors).

Unlike the rather diffuse image of the new man, none of our respondents had any difficulty in identifying the characteristics of the new lad, reeling off a familiar list of traits and consumer goods: 'beer, shoes, cars, stereos and women' (Sheffield 18-year-olds); 'big chunky watches, suits, haircuts' (Bristol lecturers); 'beer, football, women, clothes, music and films' and later, 'football, booze, women, films, what was the other one?' (Sheffield postgraduates). The list of characteristics [...] was sometimes qualified, as in the following discussion:

Eddie: I think [the magazines] are aimed at the average lad ... have a few beers, watch the footie, trying to, er, pull girls [laughs] ...

Tom: It's like getting away from the 'new man' image.

Eddie: But at the same time it's not going back to like the ...

Tom: It's like you've got to look good, but you've still got to have your traditional attitudes, like having beers and watching footie ... you can go out and have a good laugh, a few beers, but also, like, be civil you know, like sensitive (Sheffield 18-year-olds).

The apparent ambiguity of contemporary masculinities was taken up by several other groups, describing forms of masculinity that were 'not sexist, not racist but interested in drinking, getting drunk' (Sheffield disabled men) or 'being a boy, liking your beer, but also being quite aware, do you know what I mean? It's OK to be a bit of a lad ... [but] you can have your politics and respect for women' (Sheffield postgraduates).

If laddish masculinity was only too 'natural' for some men, others were grateful for the support that the men's magazines gave them in legitimising behaviour that might previously have been criticised. Whereas, previously, men had been in constant danger of 'slipping up and making some mistake' (Derby men), there was now more cultural approval for 'being yourself'. The magazines have played a crucial role in this: 'giving you permission ... to be the man you want to be ... you know, whether I want to start screwing around or whatever ... it's OK to be actually who I am' (Islington professionals); 'it's sort of allowing you to say and talk about things that you might have thought but you didn't really talk about too much and you might feel slightly embarrassed about' (Manchester lecturers). In response to this widely felt sense of insecurity, the magazines were seen to offer something 'like a palliative for all the things that you're unsure about' (Pimlico graduates). The magazines were there 'to assure your identity ... how you're supposed to look' (Sheffield disabled men); their success 'plays upon those things that you're going to feel inadequate about ... because you want to make up the deficit' (Stoke Newington media professionals); 'you need that kind of support' (Bristol musicians and artists).

The repertoires of 'honesty' and 'naturalness' are also significant in that they imply the existence of a more balanced form of masculinity – in between the extremes of the new man and the new lad – neither a traditional form of masculinity nor a simple response to the alleged extremes of feminism and political correctness (discussed below). This more 'authentic' form of masculinity was felt by some groups (e.g. Bristol students) to be most closely approximated in *Loaded* (in terms of its 'honesty' and lack of pretentiousness). Other groups felt that such balance was potentially available in new and more open forms of masculinity, an opportunity that had failed to materialise or a moment that had been lost (e.g. Stoke Newington media professionals).

[...] While some participants were critical of the magazines' celebration of laddish masculinities, many more revelled in the lack of restraint implied by what they construed as a return to more 'natural' expressions of masculinity, including, for example, the opportunity to look at pictures of sexy women in an unself-conscious and relatively guilt-free way. The Sheffield postgraduates argued that *Loaded* 'does something dead simple', reflecting 'how blokes are'. While images of the new man were commonly recognised as a cultural construction, laddish forms of masculinity were generally regarded as more 'honest' and 'natural'. As one of the Manchester lecturers suggested: 'New Laddism is a sort of honest and open view about blokes between the ages of 17 and 35'. By the late 1990s, then, laddishness had become so taken-for-granted as a form of masculinity that it was widely regarded as 'natural', in contrast to other versions of masculinity, such as the new man, which were commonly perceived to be a media construction.

'Openness'

Returning to a more 'honest' or 'natural' expression of men's true selves is partly contradicted by some of the magazines' encouragement of a greater sense of 'openness' to new forms of masculinity. Magazines such as *Men's Health*, for example, encourage men to be more open about themselves (to talk about their feelings, for example), while bringing out into the open certain (previously repressed) aspects of masculinity, including more public discussion of men's relationships, fashion and health. However, the magazines constantly monitor this process, using humour and other devices to help distance their readers from any embarrassment that they might feel at being seen to take these issues too seriously.

Expressing 'openness' about sexuality raised particular problems for the magazines and for the men in our focus groups. While the magazines are dominated by images of sexy young women, their fashion pages also provide readers with a publicly acceptable way of looking at images of beautiful young men without the stigma that attaches to reading or viewing more explicitly homoerotic images: 'most gay magazines you couldn't read [in public, but] I wouldn't feel embarrassed reading this on the train'; 'there's lots of gorgeous blokes in it and perhaps they appeal to both [gay and straight] markets, you know' (Sheffield gay men). While, for some readers, the magazines might open up a space to desire differently, in other respects they simply reinscribe traditional notions of gender and sexual difference ('Who's gay, who's straight?' *Maxim*, January 1997). Apart from the sheer predominance of female models in the magazines, the fashion sections that feature male models are usually relegated to the back pages. Even there, male models tend to be shot in very active, sporting poses (doing kung fu or judo kicks, for example) or alongside female models, apparently confirming their heterosexuality. As one reader argued:

> [T]hey've managed very subtly to avoid the gay ... because there is a hetero and gay distinction here ... but it's absolutely [clear], you know, these are guys' guys, this is about a hetero guy. It's quite interesting the way that that's been stressed and a lot of taboos have been very very carefully scooted around. (Stoke Newington media professionals)

Other readers were more ambivalent about representations of sexuality in the magazines, talking about having 'a sneaky glance' and referring to their 'illicit aspect' (Pimlico graduates). One participant worried about reading *Men's Health* on the bus while travelling through Manchester's gay village, fearing that people would assume he was gay. More common, however, was the suggestion that 'gay people have led fashion in our lifetimes and we can see that the gap between the straight scene and the gay scene has sort of closed' (Sheffield gay men). Nor was this view restricted to gay men. Whereas men were previously 'very coy', now they were 'opening up' (London art college students); 'I think people are more open, it's socially more acceptable to say that you are different, you can sort of desire openly as a man' (Bristol lecturers).

One of the key ways in which the magazines handle the tension between the need for men to be more open while maintaining their traditional (gendered and sexually stereotyped) notions of masculinity is through the use of humour. So, too, in our focus groups, humour was often used to return the conversation to safer ground following a discussion of emotional relationships, personal problems or sexuality [...]   A similar argument applies to the repertoire of 'harmless fun' which is mobilised in opposition to those who take the magazines too seriously, rather than reading them for a laugh. This same repertoire can also be deployed against those who find the magazines offensive, verging on pornography.

Reading source

Jackson et al., 2001, pp.116–21   ■ ■ ■

Reading 4.2 examined different discourses of *honesty, naturalness* and *openness* in men's discussions of the magazines and masculinity to give a sense of the different discourses that people in the focus groups moved between. The men largely affirmed the culture of the magazines, but in these different discourses Jackson et al. found a large degree of *ambivalence*. Media constructions of 'laddishness' have come to seem so 'natural' that for many respondents there was no need to defend them or to consider alternative forms of masculinity. While some participants were critical of the magazines' celebration of 'laddish' masculinities, many more revelled in the lack of restraint implied by, as they saw it, a return to more 'natural' expressions of masculinity, including, for example, the opportunity to look at pictures of 'sexy' women in an unself-conscious and relatively guilt-free way. However, the discourses of both 'honesty' and 'naturalness' were partly contradicted by some of the magazines' encouragement of a greater sense of 'openness' to new forms of masculinity. The men interviewed also identified the role the magazines played in 'unfixing' masculinity, by generally broadening the different ways there are of 'being a man'. The magazines encouraged men to be more 'open' about themselves (to talk about their feelings, for example), while bringing out certain (previously repressed) aspects of masculinity including more public discussion of men's relationships, fashion and health. However, the magazines constantly monitor this process, using humour and other devices to help 'distance' readers from any embarrassment they might feel at being seen to take these issues 'too seriously'.

Although this is not apparent in Reading 4.2 above, this ambivalence about masculinity is also evident in the sorts of celebrities that were featured by the magazines. The invention of the category of the 'new lad' meant that many of the magazines often represented masculine icons from the 1970s. These included footballers such as George Best and Rodney Marsh, and actors such as Phil Daniels (star of the 1979 film *Quadrophenia*). The 1970s signified a male heterosexual utopia before what many of the men interviewed and the magazines identified as the advent of 'political correctness' and castrating forms of feminism. The magazines exhibited nostalgia for a time when straight masculinity was perceived to be less regulated than more contemporary periods. However, on the other hand – and here again we see ambivalence – the magazines regularly featured 'softer' forms of masculinity evident in pictures of footballer David Beckham, Jarvis Cocker (lead singer of the rock group Pulp) and Damon Albarn (lead singer of the rock group Blur), although in fact the emphasis was usually placed on their laddish credentials. The idea of the lad depended upon an ideological contradiction. Again what is important here is less the way actual celebrities appear in the magazines, but how they are constructed by a number of discourses associated with laddishness. The men's magazines, then, were simultaneously involved in processes of masculinisation and feminisation. The contradiction they sought to magically resolve was how to be masculine and to be concerned about your clothes and appearance without running the risk of being thought of as gay. Given our analysis it is difficult to understand young men's reactions to these magazines as blasé (they mostly expressed themselves enthusiastically) or as an unambiguous form of resistance. This potentially takes us beyond the very positive reading of media, celebrity and audience suggested by the work of Stacey and Fiske, but also suggests the limits of studies that claim most media consumption is casual, distracted and trivial.

Further, it is worth noting that the enthusiasm of the men involved in the project came not from their position as fans, but as ordinary consumers. This complicates our understanding of ordinary people's reaction to celebrities in a number of ways. First, it is not only fans who are capable of enthusiastic reactions to the celebrities they watch, read about and listen to. Second, we need to be careful not to assume that enthusiasm on the part of the consumers of celebrities is always an unambiguous form of resistance towards the dominant culture. In this respect, audience 'activity' can indeed offer strategies for resistance, but it can equally reaffirm dominant social relations on the basis of class, 'race', gender and sexuality, for example. In terms of the study by Jackson et al., celebrities and stars are positioned within certain discourses that are then drawn upon by young men to 'make sense of' or 'handle' contemporary social changes in gender relations. The study of celebrity remains tied to an understanding of the operation of the media industries, and of strategies of resistance, but perhaps more significantly it is also linked to ways of understanding social transformations in society. Celebrities become figures in which we invest, in order to give meaning to our lives, but also to help us deal with changing social and cultural values.

5.3 Gender and identification

Spend a minute thinking back to Jackie Stacey's argument about women's identifications with (female) film stars (see Section 3). How does this compare with Jackson et al.'s study of a male readership's identification with men's magazines? ■ ■ ■

The question of 'identification' raised by Stacey is key to the study by Jackson et al., but it is handled in a different way. It is argued that young men (and some young women) exhibit a mostly enthusiastic disposition towards the magazines because they are a way of making sense of gender transformation. In terms of masculinity, the more 'certain' world of patriarchal relations between men and women is not only part of a wider nostalgia that protects men's material interests, but also a reaction against a number of changes which have served to destabilise modern masculine identities: the economic transformation of women's position; the increased visibility of diverse sexualities such as gay and lesbian groups; and the social and political impact of feminism. The combination of 'soft' and 'laddish' representations of masculinity enables male consumers to move between a number of different positions within the magazines' content in terms of the repertoires and discourses used in talking about the magazines. That the magazines allow for a number of different discursive positions best accounts for their success.

The wider implication of the study is that our relationships with well-known personalities is largely ordered and mediated by already existing powerful discourses – in this case on masculinity and gender. However, it also argues that we should be careful to avoid the assumption that such discourses are monolithic as they are negotiated in complex ways by different groups of men and women. The diverse, shifting and contradictory sets of identifications exhibited by our focus groups suggest that constructionist accounts of celebrity may offer more subtle forms of analysis than presumptions of either resistance or compliance.

However, there may be dangers in the stress on ambivalence. We could end up going so far into the ambivalent sensibilities of modern consumers that we forget that mediated celebrity would not exist unless backed by powerful institutions and forms of cultural power (see Chapter 3). What is sometimes absent from the analysis is the connection between cultures of celebrity and dominant patterns of consumer narcissism that are inevitably built upon cultures of profit and exploitation (I recognise that my own work, as discussed above, is vulnerable to this criticism). However, the recent developments discussed above suggest that a return to the moralising critique that characterised some aspects of earlier waves of theorising is highly undesirable.

6 Conclusion

We have seen over the course of this chapter how the study of media, audiences and celebrity has changed. Gone it seems are the sweeping generalisations about the duping of the masses to be found in the work of Adorno and Horkheimer. We saw that Dyer offers a very different reading of stardom, also based on the notion of charisma, but recognising the positive and transformative potential of mass mediated celebrities. The idea of 'reading' audience responses directly from texts has continued in many areas of academic life, and in media studies it has been complemented by a great deal of empirical work such as interviews and other methods, which aims to engage with the way that audiences actually understand texts. This was illustrated in the work of Jackie Stacey discussed in Section 3. Stacey's study was also used to show that such empirical work is often tied to optimistic understandings of audiences and what they *do with* media, in line with Dyer's work, but in complete contradiction to Adorno and Horkheimer. It is worth pointing out again here that, in many ways, the writers discussed are, to various degrees, representative of wider currents of fashion in the study of media at the time they were writing. We saw in Section 4 that John Fiske carries Stacey and Dyer's optimism even further with his analysis of fans. This approach was characterised as a cultural studies approach, because of the association of much cultural studies with this very optimistic reading of fan and other audience activity – though it is important to say that many researchers in cultural and media studies have been critical of this approach. In the final section, we saw that more recent work on media, audiences and celebrity in media and cultural studies has sought to locate contemporary audiences in more complex frameworks, stressing ambivalence and the co-existence of complex discourses. This constructionist approach is based on a study of specific audiences and readerships, instead of choosing between optimistic and pessimistic understandings of the audience abstracted from its social context.

Further reading

Alasuutari, P. (1999) 'Introduction: three phases of reception studies' in Alasuutari, P. (ed.) *The Media Audience*, London, Sage.

Dyer, R. (1998) *Stars*, London, British Film Institute.

Ehrenreich, B., Hess, E. and Jacobs, G. (1991) 'Beatlemania: girls just want to have fun' in Lewis, L. (ed.) *The Adoring Audience: Fan Culture and Popular Media*, London, Routledge.

Fiske, J. (1991) 'The cultural economy of fandom' in Lewis, L. (ed.) *The Adoring Audience: Fan Culture and Popular Media*, London, Routledge.

Hermes, J. (1999) 'Media figures in identity construction' in Alasuutari, P. (ed.) *Rethinking the Media Audience*, London, Sage.

Jackson, P., Stevenson, N. and Brooks, K. (2001) *Making Sense of Men's Magazines*, Cambridge, Polity Press.

Kellner, D. (1995) *Media Culture*, London, Routledge.

Stacey, J. (1994) *Star Gazing: Hollywood Cinema and Female Spectatorship*, London, Routledge.

Thompson, J.B. (1990) *Ideology and Modern Culture*, Cambridge, Polity Press.

References

Adorno, T. (1991) *The Culture Industry: Selected Essays on Mass Culture* (edited by J. Bernstein), London, Routledge.

Adorno, T. and Horkheimer, M. (1979, first published in 1944) 'The culture industry: enlightenment as mass deception' in *Dialectic of Enlightenment,* London, Verso.

Alasuutari, P. (1999) 'Introduction: three phases of reception studies' in Alasuutari, P. (ed.) *The Media Audience*, London, Sage.

Alberoni, F. (1972) 'The powerless elite' in McQuail, D. (ed.) *Sociology of Mass Communications*, London, Penguin.

Bourdieu, P. (1984) *Distinction*, London, Routledge.

Dyer, R. (1998) *Stars*, London, British Film Institute.

de Certeau, M. (1984) *The Practice of Everyday Life*, Berkeley, CA, University of California Press.

Ehrenreich, B., Hess, E. and Jacobs, G. (1991) 'Beatlemania: girls just want to have fun' in Lewis, L. (ed.) *The Adoring Audience: Fan Culture and Popular Media*, London, Routledge.

Fiske, J. (1989a) *Understanding Popular Culture*, London, Unwin Hyman.

Fiske, J. (1989b) *Reading the Popular*, London, Unwin Hyman.

Fiske, J. (1991) 'The cultural economy of fandom' in Lewis, L. (ed.) *The Adoring Audience: Fan Culture and Popular Media*, London, Routledge.

Hall, S. (1980) 'Encoding/Decoding' in Hall, S., Hobson, D., Lowe, A. and Willis, P. (eds) *Culture, Media, Language*, London, Hutchinson.

Hermes, J. (1995) *Reading Women's Magazines*, Cambridge, Polity Press.

Hermes, J. (1999) 'Media figures in identity construction' in Alasuutari, P. (ed.) *Rethinking the Media Audience*, London, Sage.

Jackson, P., Stevenson, N. and Brooks, K. (2001) *Making Sense of Men's Magazines*, Cambridge, Polity Press.

Johnson, P. (1964) 'The menace of Beatlism', *New Statesman*, 28 February.

Kellner, D. (1995) *Media Culture*, London, Routledge.

Stacey, J. (1994) *Star Gazing: Hollywood Cinema and Female Spectatorship*, London, Routledge.

Simmel, G. (1997, first published in 1903) 'The metropolis and mental life' in Frisby, D. and Featherstone, M. (eds) *Simmel on Culture: Selected Writings*, London, Sage.

Thompson, J.B. (1990) *Ideology and Modern Culture*, Cambridge, Polity Press.

Weber, M. (1968) *Economy and Society: An Outline of Interpretive Sociology* (edited by G. Roth and C. Wittich), New York, Bedminster Press

Mediated celebrity: linking texts, producers and audiences

Conclusion

Jessica Evans

Throughout this book we have examined how each conceptual element – production, text and reception – can contribute in its own right to *making celebrity a meaningful social entity*. In the conclusion, we consider how we can interpret the relationships *between* these elements.

As we have seen, celebrity means much more than the actual person who is represented textually. Celebrity is a 'sign' that represents individuals – something that we have called 'mediated personae' – who are given heightened significance through mass circulation in the social world (Marshall, 1997). Further, these personae are brought into our homes and everyday lives – via magazines, television, films and the internet – by the highly structured efforts of a range of media industries. Bringing historical research to bear on these elements, as Chapter 1 showed, is also important. This is because the relationships between producers, the texts they create and the audiences who receive them may change over time. For instance, the relationship between audiences and producers is altered by the technical means of dissemination. Furthermore, historical evidence indicates that, as well as important recent changes, long-term continuities also exist in celebrity texts. As a result, it can be shown that some of the values and meanings we associate with celebrity today were clearly present at earlier historical periods, and the actual category of 'star' or 'celebrity' emerges in particular institutional, economic and cultural contexts.

It is often argued that there is a series of discrete steps whereby producers make media artefacts that are subsequently marketed and, as a further or secondary stage, consumed or received by audiences. As we have mentioned, 'mass culture' theorists (Adorno and Horkheimer, 1979/1944) have tended to see this as a chain of cause and effect (see Introduction and Chapter 4). It is thought that power lies only with the producers and that audiences simply believe in the ideologies or value systems producers create. It is also assumed that the texts created by media organisations merely reflect producers' conscious attempts to manipulate audiences. It is interesting to note that frequently commercial media organisations tend to think about supply and demand in this causal way too. In their case, however, the chain of events begins with demand. So, typically, in justification of their output, media companies argue that the media only reflect demand and audiences get the media they want or that they feature celebrity in newspapers because everyone is fascinated by celebrity and wants to know all about celebrities' lives.

This 'causal' or 'reflectionist' approach perhaps simplifies the complexity of what really happens. One argument against this approach stresses the relative independence of the domains of production, textual meaning and reception. For example, we may agree that much resource within the media industries goes into controlling risk. As Chapter 3 showed, strategies of market integration and formatting aim to target a product to the right media markets and thus a potential audience that will respond in predictable ways. However, risk management is not an absolute science, but a matter of interpretation. Media texts do not necessarily reflect in any simple and direct way the intentions of individual producers. As Chapter 2's study of textual communication stresses, texts involve their own habitual systems of meaning-making, using codes and conventions, and collectively form genres. Neither producers nor audiences are always consciously aware of the structures that allow these meanings to be made: the conventions of texts to a large extent pre-exist any one media producer, who may nonetheless deploy them. Rarely does any individual or organisation invent them, although new combinations are always being created. Moreover, while producers might mean to 'encode' a text in a certain way, so as to procure a 'preferred' reading from their target audience, in actuality audiences and individual viewers may make sense of it, or 'decode' it in unexpected ways (see Chapters 2 and 4). Thus, to some extent, as Chapter 4 argued, the 'decoding' (interpretation) work that involves audiences needs to be regarded as a practice in its own right.

However, there are also ways in which the domains of production, text and reception intertwine or shape each other. For example, the construction of a film star's persona as it appears in the film text is not a secondary process, worked out film by film, nor is it solely a matter of post-production marketing strategy. Since 1914 (deCordova, 1991), it has been integral to the way that films or any other media product involving stars get made and categorised into different types or genres (Wyatt, 1994; see the discussion on formatting in Chapter 3, Section 3). Furthermore, producers take heed of audiences' responses to their products via market research and build these into the planning of new products. Film and television producers, for example, select actors on the basis of the market they will attract, and this is dependent on their persona. Celebrity is, then, a marketing device and market testing is built into the pre-production stage. Moreover, a particular star or celebrity may generate unpredictable forms of identification from certain audiences and their persona will be modified accordingly (as you will remember from the discussion on Kylie Minogue in Chapter 2). Others may intentionally alter their persona by moving into different genres, formats, or media.

Often these mutations in persona arise through 'secondary texts' (such as gossip columns), not only through 'primary texts' (the 'core' texts that represent the professional work of the star concerned) – a distinction that you may remember from Chapter 2, Section 3.3. For example, Michelle Collins, the actor discussed in Chapter 1, one of Oxfam's long-haul celebrities, is now shifting from populist, working-class media coverage by acting in serious post-watershed drama programmes (her core text). Consequently, Oxfam expect her to win more middle-class media interest, in secondary texts such as women's monthly (rather than weekly) magazines and upmarket newspapers (Evans, 2003).

This distinction between core and secondary texts is a useful analytical device because it helps us to classify different media texts according to their function. However, distinguishing between them is not always straightforward; neither are they necessarily dependent on, or consistent with, each other. So, for example, celebrities may appear in what could be defined as a secondary text even when there is no 'core' text, that is when there is no obvious 'work' to promote (see Chapter 2, Section 3.3). For some, this feature of celebrity is a very contemporary one, and provides evidence for Boorstin's argument that today's celebrity is a 'person who is known for his well-knownness' (Boorstin, 1961, p.57; see Chapter 1). But, leaving aside the question of whether this has always been a feature of celebrity (a matter discussed in Chapter 1), it can be said that media producers, celebrities and audiences are involved in a more *or less continuous activity* of engagement with meanings and interpretations across a whole range of media texts whose meanings interlock.

There are, then, a number of approaches to the question of how texts, producers and audiences are related (for further discussion of these concepts see **Gillespie, 2005; Hesmondhalgh, 2006; Gillespie and Toynbee, 2006**). One thing is certain: there can be no absolute and for-all-time answer to the question of their relationship – it all depends on which media, at which historical moment, which mode of dissemination (one-to-one, one-to-many), what kinds of audience and so on. It is always important to take into account the fact that centralised producers do indeed have great command of resources and are able to a large extent to control the means of dissemination of media messages, as well as their content. However, this does not mean that we can assume that media producers have ultimate control over the meanings circulated by the media. While we may enjoy flicking through *Hello!*, does this mean that we have a straightforward, unambivalent relationship to what we are looking at? We hope that, having completed your journey 'inside celebrity', you now have a good understanding of why it is so vital to study the media.

References

Adorno, T. and Horkheimer, M. (1979/1944) 'The culture industry: enlightenment as mass deception' in Adorno, T. and Horkheimer, M. (eds) *Dialectic of Enlightenment*, London, Verso.

Boorstin, D. (1961) *The Image: A Guide to Pseudo-Events in America*, Harmondsworth, Penguin.

deCordova, R. (1991) 'The emergence of the star system in America' in Gledhill, C. (ed.) *Stardom: Industry of Desire*, London, Routledge.

Evans, J. (2003) Interview conducted with Claire Lewis, Celebrity Co-ordinator in Oxfam's Media Unit, Oxford, April.

Gillespie, M. (ed.) (2005) *Media Audiences*, Maidenhead, Open University Press/The Open University (Book 2 in this series).

Gillespie, M. and Toynbee, J. (eds) (2006) *Analysing Media Texts*, Maidenhead, Open University Press/The Open University (Book 4 in this series).

Hesmondhalgh, D. (ed.) (2006) *Media Production*, Maidenhead, Open University Press/The Open University (Book 3 in this series).

Marshall, P.D. (1997) *Celebrity and Power: Fame in Contemporary Society*, Minneapolis, MN, University of Minnesota Press.

Wyatt, J. (1994) *High Concept: Cinema and Marketing in Hollywood*, Austin, TX, University of Texas Press.

Acknowledgements

Grateful acknowledgement is made to the following sources for permission to reproduce material within this product.

Chapter 1

Figures

Figure 1.1: Copyright © Dave Gaskill; Figure 1.2: Copyright © The British Museum; Figure 1.3: © Photo SCALA, Florence, Galleria Sabauda, Turin (1992) – courtesy of the Ministero Beni e Att. Culturali; Figure 1.8: Clarkson, M. (2000) Angel Michelle, Manchester Evening News, 10 April 2000. Copyright © MEN Syndication; Figure 1.9: Michelle Collins in Brazil, Hello!, 14 March 2000, Hello Ltd. Photographs © Scope Features; Figure 1.10: Morris, N. and Russell, B. (2004) Blair admits he did not know 45-minute claim referred to battlefield; weapons, The Independent, 5 February 2004. Photograph by Gretel Ensignia.

Readings

Reading 1.1: de Cordova, R. (1985) The emergence of the star system in America, Wide Angle, Vol. 6, No. 4, Ohio University School of Film.

Chapter 2

Figures

Figure 2.1: Copyright © Phil Hillyard / Newspix; Figure 2.2: Copyright © SIPA / Rex Features; Figure 2.3: Copyright © Gregg De Guire / Wireimage; Figure 2.4: Courtesy of Ford Motor Company UK; Figure 2.5 (a): Cover artwork of 'Kylie' by Kylie Minogue used by permission of Pete Waterman Ltd; Figure 2.5 (b): Cover artwork for 'Fever' and 'Body language' by Kylie Minogue used by permission of EMI Records; Figure 2.5 (c): Cover artwork for 'Kylie Minogue' used by permission of BMG UK & Ireland Ltd; Figure 2.5 (d): Cover artwork for 'Fever' and 'Body Language' by Kylie Minogue used by permission of EMI Records.

Readings

Reading 2.2: Neale, S. (1990) Questions of Genre, Screen, Vol. 31:1 Spring 1990. By permission of Screen; Reading 2.3: Connell, I., Personalities in the popular media, in Dahlgren, P. and Sparks, C. (eds) (1992) Journalism and Popular Culture. Reprinted by permission of Sage Publications Ltd.

Chapter 3

Figures

Figure 3.1: Copyright © Michael Tweed / Associated Press; Figure 3.2: Donnelly, C. (2003) I was a Full Monty star ... Then road accident sent my world crashing, Daily Mirror, 19 March 2003. Copyright © Mirrorpix. Main image by Phil Spencer; Figure 3.3: Copyright © Channel Four Films / Ronald Grant Archive; Figure 3.4: Copyright © Paramount Pictures / Ronald Grant Archive; Figure 3.5: Copyright © Universal Pictures / Ronald Grant Archive; Figure 3.6: Copyright © Rex Features.

Readings

Reading 3.2: Donelly, C. (2003) I was a Full Monty star .... Then road accident sent my world crashing, Daily Mirror, 19 March 2003. Copyright © Mirrorpix.

Chapter 4

Figures

Figure 4.1: Copyright © Sharok Hatami / Rex Features; Figure 4.2: Copyright © Rex Features; Figure 4.3: Copyright © Sam Shaw / Rex Features; Figures 4.4, 4.5, 4.6: Courtesy of the British Film Institute; Figure 4.7: Copyright © Twentieth Century Fox Film. Courtesy of the British Film Institute; Figure 4.8 (a): Copyright © Everett Collection / Rex Features; Figure 4.8 (b): Copyright © John Roca / Rex Features.

Readings

Reading 4.1: Stacey, J. (1994) Star Gazing: Hollywood Cinema and Female Spectatorship, Routledge, Taylor and Francis Books Ltd, www.tandf.co.uk & www.eBookstore.tandf.co.uk; Reading 4.2: Jackson, P., 'Honesty', Naturalness' and 'Openness' in Jackson, P., Stevenson, L. and Brooks, K. (eds) (2001) Making Sense of Men's magazines, Polity Press.

Colour section

Plate 1: Copyright © Eddie Adams; Plate 2: Mastercuts, Beechwood Music Ltd, 1997; Plate 3: MCA Records Ltd, 1991; Plate 4: Universal – Island Records, 2001; Plate 5: Sony Music Entertainment Inc., 1996; Plates 6 & 7: Food Ltd, EMI Records Ltd, 1994; Plate 8: American Media, Inc. Reprinted with permission; Plates 9 and 10: Newsweek, 3 July 1995 © 1995 Newsweek, Inc. All rights reserved. Reprinted by permission. Photos © Eddie Adams; Plates 11a & 11b: Claire Goose: The TV star's personal diary of her visit to Ethiopia to meet the coffee farmers who are facing tragedy, Hello!; November 2002, Hello Limited. Photos © Scope Features; Plate 12: Copyright © Warner Bros / Ronald Grant Archive.

Cover image
© Georges Blanc, Camera Press, London.

Every effort has been made to contact copyright holders. If any have been inadvertently overlooked the publishers will be pleased to make the necessary arrangements at the first opportunity.

Index